HOW TO READ A PERSON LIKE A BOOK

OBSERVING BODY LANGUAGE TO KNOW WHAT PEOPLE ARE THINKING

GERARD I. NIERENBERG

HENRY H. CALERO

GABRIEL GRAYSON

SQUAREONE
PUBLISHERS

Cover Designer: Jeannie Tudor
Cover Photo: Getty Images, Inc.
Interior Illustrations: Cathy Morrison
Editor: Danielle Burby and Joanne Abrams
Typesetter: Terry Wiscovitch

Square One Publishers
115 Herricks Road
Garden City Park, NY 11040
(516) 535-2010 • (877) 900-BOOK
www.squareonepublishers.com

Library of Congress Cataloging-in-Publication Data

Nierenberg, Gerard I.
  How to read a person like a book : observing body language to know what people are thinking / Gerard I. Nierenberg, Henry H. Calero, Gabriel Grayson.
    p. cm.
  Includes bibliographical references and index.
  ISBN 978-0-7570-0314-1 (pbk.)
  1. Body language. I. Calero, Henry H. II. Grayson, Gabriel. III. Title.

BF637.N66N54 2010
153.6'9—dc22

2009035793

Printed in the United States of America

10   9   8   7   6   5   4   3   2   1

Contents

To Juliet and Yen.

–Jerry and Hank

*To my conspicuously
wonderful sister,
Mary Ann.*

–Gabe

Preface

The first edition of this book and the research behind it occurred long before the term "body language" became commonplace. The idea for this book originated in the early 1960s when coauthor Henry "Hank" Calero purchased a videotape-recording system for use in his business seminars. At the time, Hank was conducting programs for executives and managers in the AeroSpace Industry in California. He designed mock-negotiation case studies in which the attendees would role-play for the camera so that he could later analyze the material. In a matter of a few months, Hank had accumulated a wealth of nonverbal information. His realization that gestures, postures, and expressions were silently communicating every emotion—from authority and confidence to defensiveness and self-consciousness—was revolutionary at the time. He began discussing nonverbal communication at his seminars and found that his attendees and people who had heard about his research were greatly interested. Soon, he teamed up with the man dubbed the Father of Negotiating by *Forbes* magazine, Gerard "Jerry" Nierenberg, author of the best-selling book *The Art of Negotiating*. After much additional research, Hank and Jerry wrote the original *How to Read a Person Like a Book*.

It's been nearly forty years since the publication of *How to Read a Person Like a Book*, and since that time, the sheer amount of knowledge that has accumulated on the subject of body language has been overwhelming—or at least it may seem so to the untrained. Fortunately, this book is intended to bring you back to the basics, to the roots, to make "reading a person like a book" as uncomplicated as it sounds. Joining the authors for this new edition of *How to Read a Person Like a Book* is Gabriel Grayson, author of the number-one sign language book in America, *Talking with Your Hands, Listening with Your Eyes*. As chair of the sign language and nonverbal communications department of the New School of General Studies in New York City, as well as the son of deaf parents, Gabe brings a very unique understanding of body language to the table. Together, the authors have updated the information presented in these pages without compromising its original accessibility and integrity.

A final note on the text is in order. In an effort to avoid lengthy and awkward phrasing within sentences, it is our style to alternate the use of generic male and female pronouns according to section. Therefore, one discussion employs the female "she" and "her" pronouns, while the next uses the male "he" and "his" pronouns. Hopefully, this provides an unbiased and easy-to-read text.

How to Read a Person Like a Book is sure to become an important tool in your ongoing search for a more complete way to understand the feelings, attitudes, and behaviors of others. If used properly, this knowledge will allow you to create more rewarding personal, professional, and casual relationships.

Introduction

*"By a man's fingernails, by his coat-sleeve, by his boots,
by his trouser-knees, by the calluses of his forefinger and thumb,
by his expression, by his shirt-cuffs, by his movements—
by each of these things a man's calling is plainly revealed."*

—Sir Arthur Conan Doyle, *A Study in Scarlet*

eople-watching always proves to be a fascinating diversion. You've probably done it from time to time at the mall, at the grocery store, in meetings, during social gatherings, at sporting events, and so on. And if you're like us, you've probably found yourself wondering what someone was thinking—what the story was behind a certain action or decision.

You probably already know that the "faces" people make or the way they tilt their heads, for instance, suggest certain thoughts or feelings. What people convey with their bodies, regardless of whether or not any words are said, speaks volumes about their intentions and emotions. And if words are spoken, knowing what a person is communicating via body language can, in many cases, help affirm or contradict what you are hearing.

Being aware of the emotions and intentions behind certain mannerisms can help you in all areas of your life. The more you practice "reading people like a book," the more you'll understand what makes them tick. With this deeper understanding, you'll be able to deal more effectively with people on a professional, personal, and casual level.

By reading this book, you'll learn how to train yourself to pay attention to the nonverbal language going on all around you. You'll begin to "listen" with your eyes, watching carefully for the words, sentences, and paragraphs people write with their gestures and expressions. In Chapter 1, you'll train yourself to become a keen observer of people. Then, in Chapter 2, you'll come face to face with the expressions people make and the meanings behind them. The rest of the body plays as much of a role in nonverbal communication as the face, so in Chapter 3, you'll learn the individual meanings of body gestures. You know that individual words do not convey a complete thought; even a sentence leaves many things unsaid. In much the same way, expressions and body gestures need to be strung together to provide a more complete picture of someone's feelings or intentions. Therefore, Chapter 4 examines various attitudes along with the gesture clusters that are common to them. Finally, Chapter 5 takes a look at body language and relationships. In that important chapter, you'll see how the gestures you've already learned about may surface in interactions with your child, your romantic partner, your staff, and other significant people in your life, and you'll discover how you can employ your own body language to enhance these relationships.

You can learn a lot by reading body language, but please take this brief warning to heart: It's easy to believe that you have a good grasp of nonverbal communication after just a bit of exposure, but it's a mistake to become complacent. Be careful not to jump to conclusions based on some light reading and practice. Gaining a deeper understanding of people through studying their behaviors should be a lifelong learning experience, so don't try to figure everything out all at once. Instead, focus on something new each day, or even each week, depending on the complexity of the behavior or person. Indeed, each hour you spend consciously observing body language is merely a small step up the long staircase of knowledge. Always keep in mind that "reading a person like a book" is an observational art, not an exact science. There are many variables and interpretations to take into account, so be observant, know your material as well as your subjects, and allow room for some surprises!

1

Becoming an Avid Reader of Body Language

*"Learning is acquired by reading books, but the much more necessary
learning, the knowledge of the world, is only to be acquired by
reading men, and studying all the various editions of them."*

—The Earl of Chesterfield, *Letters to His Son*

To learn how to read a person like a book, the first thing you need to do is become a good observer. You can begin to hone your skills by going to places that are heavily populated and consciously observing the gestures, expressions, overall actions, and interactions between people. In this chapter, we'll help you set the stage for keen observation, beginning with one of the most useful places to sharpen your abilities, the airport. We'll discuss what you should look for to help you increase your awareness. In later chapters, you'll start to learn the body's vocabulary and how to recognize "sentences" and "paragraphs" to figure out the likely meanings.

YOUR OBSERVATION DECK: THE AIRPORT

An airport is an excellent place to view the entire human spectrum of behavior. It is a wonderful laboratory for observing a myriad of nonverbal messages that can reveal thoughts, feelings, and attitudes. While watching travelers arriving and departing, you can guess what they are feeling by observing their body language. You can determine if they are concerned about missing a flight, anticipating a good visit with friends and family, or wondering whether or not someone will be there to pick them up, among other things.

Here's an example: A businesswoman is seated at the terminal waiting for her flight to be called. You note that her body is upright and rigid, her back is stiff, her ankles are locked, and her hands are clenched. (See Figure 1.1.) You may determine from this nonverbal message that she is nervous and concerned. You might deduce that she has a fear of flying or perhaps that her flight is delayed and she is concerned. Maybe she'll miss an important appointment at her destination.

Figure 1.1.

The Nervous Businesswoman.

Further along, you see three businessmen talking on their cell phones. You observe that the first man is tensely seated, staring at the laptop computer in front of him. His shoulders are rigid; his jacket is buttoned, as if he's going to a meeting; and his facial expression is serious. (See Figure 1.2.) You determine that this man is likely speaking to someone whom he wants to impress, convince, or influence in some manner—possibly, his boss.

Figure 1.2.
The All-Business
Businessman.

The second man you encounter is considerably more relaxed. He has one leg casually crossed over the other, and one hand held behind his head as he leans back slightly. His smiling expression and easygoing attitude makes you feel that he is talking to a good friend or, perhaps, to his wife. (See Figure 1.3.)

Figure 1.3.
The Relaxed
Businessman.

The third man you see is speaking into his phone in hushed tones as he hunches forward, trying to create some privacy in the crowded airport. (See Figure 1.4.) You note that one hand is held like a shield on the left side of his face, as if he's screening his expression from the view of others, and his eyes are cast downward. By reading his body language, you conclude that he is being secretive. Perhaps he is planning some underhanded deal or encounter.

Figure 1.4.

The Secretive Businessman.

Arriving in the baggage claim area, you see a family. Families are easily identified by their members' proximity to one another and the manner in which they walk and hold themselves, as well as their similar facial features. Watch them carefully. Are they looking forward to a great vacation together or is there tension between them, indicating that there is a less enjoyable reason for their trip? Use your intuition.

Depending on the day of the week, you may observe several travelers being greeted by family and friends; perhaps you will witness a lot of hugging and kissing. These are physical, nonverbal expressions of love and joy. Perhaps you will see other travelers who just collect their baggage and walk toward the long-term parking lot or to the curb for car service. Note whether they walk quickly or leisurely. The speed with which someone moves can give you insight into the importance of that person's trip. You will note that those who are anxiously awaiting pickup glance frequently at their watches, look down the road at the approaching vehicles, or hold their cell phones in their hand, waiting for a call.

As you can see, there are many different types of people and situations to observe at the airport. So the next time you have a long wait ahead of you, put your book or magazine down and spend some time reading people. You'll notice a wide variety of postures and gestures that will provide hints and clues about what's going on in each person's head at that moment. Go ahead and make assumptions about what he is thinking and feeling. If someone you're observing is with other people, examine how they interact with one another and take a guess as to their relationship. The more time you spend watching and interpreting, the stronger your "reading" skills will become.

VERBAL COMMUNICATION AT A GLANCE

Verbal communication does not operate in a vacuum. Indeed, it is a complex process that involves many different scenarios and intentions. While we do have an innate ability to detect how someone feels from a look, for instance, there is often a "disconnect" between what is being said and what is being revealed by the body. Our intuition tells us that something is amiss, but we may choose to ignore it or we may not trust it. Now is the time to start listening to your intuition.

When verbal and nonverbal messages conflict, it's often the case that the nonverbal gestures are more honest. Therefore, it's important for the gesture to endorse the spoken word for total and clear communication. Politicians often win or lose campaigns depending upon whether they maintain congruity in order to convey their honesty and sincerity. No doubt, many of them receive coaching to ensure that their verbal and nonverbal messages are in harmony. However, many of them still use gestures that are incongruous with what they say. An example of this would be a politician who emphatically states, "I'm sincerely receptive to a dialogue with young people," but shakes her finger at the crowd as if reprimanding them; or a politician who wants to convince the audience that he's warm, kind, and interested in their well-being but undermines his message by chopping at the air with a stiff hand to emphasize his point.

Many accomplished writers have demonstrated their understanding of the importance of verbal and nonverbal congruency in their writing. A writer must be able to paint pictures with his words. Often, pivotal scenes in novels involve a character who is hiding something and is betrayed by his own body. Sherlock Holmes, Miss Marple, and other famous literary detectives routinely use body language clues to crack the case.

It has often been said that a picture is worth a thousand words. However, we've never heard someone respond to that statement by saying, "True, but a metaphor is worth a thousand pictures." It's not. Just as we must combine what is being said with what is being displayed, we cannot take one gesture at face value without considering the other gestures we are seeing. In other words, we need to be aware of gesture clusters.

WATCH FOR GESTURE CLUSTERS

Each gesture a person makes is like a single word in a paragraph. In order to understand a language, words must be structured into units, or "sentences," which express complete thoughts. Understanding the congruence of gestures in harmony with each other takes time. Likewise, being able to isolate gestures that are incongruent in order to negate what you have perceived also requires practice. When observing someone, take into account all the words and gestures, and form complete sentences and paragraphs out of them to arrive at your conclusions. Don't take a single word or gesture at face value without considering the others. Gesture clusters will serve as monitoring devices for confirmation that you have correctly interpreted a person's attitudes. It is the same as listening to someone speak an entire sentence, rather than listening to one word, to arrive at the meaning.

For example, let's say you're talking to someone who seems capable, confident, and knowledgeable. Then, suddenly a nervous laugh escapes her lips. That nervous laugh could essentially erase your earlier observations. Perhaps she is also making quick arm and/or leg movements such as tapping or shaking, and is shifting her body as if to escape an unpleasant situation. Chances are she is not as capable, confident, or knowledgeable as you first made her out to be . . . or maybe something you just said or did made her nervous. Therefore, you also need to be aware of how your actions or words might be perceived in order to more fully understand her overall behavior.

When observing a specific gesture, look for other gestures in the cluster that have similar meanings and thereby support one another. For example, a congruent set of gestures for an anxious but enthusiastic salesperson would look like this: He's sitting on the edge of his chair with his feet wide apart, his toes pointed forward like a sprinter in a race, and his upper body leaning toward the prospective buyer. You'll learn the meanings of each of these gestures later in the book. The point here is that these gestures need to be combined to form a complete picture.

Being aware of gesture clusters will keep you from jumping to conclusions based on a few observations by forcing you to continue to observe. In other words, the awareness that there is more to read serves as "anti-assumption" control. Initially, it's fun and seems easy to read body language, but the serious student who is learning to interpret gestures quickly discovers that every movement and position can be amplified or confused by another.

The individual significance and meaning of a gesture is sometimes subject to as many interpretations as the number of people evaluating it. Therefore, you must keep in mind that a single gesture is only one nonverbal clue, and that the total message is what is important. Be careful not to be completely influenced by one movement or posture, and to base your conclusion on a preconceived notion of what you think that gesture means. Always remember that it is the total "gesture cluster" that ultimately reveals the true message.

CONSIDER THE "WHAT ELSE" FACTOR

Observing and becoming aware of gestures and postures is fairly simple. However, accurately interpreting them is quite different and much more difficult. For example, picture a woman covering her mouth while she is speaking; this would suggest that she is unsure of what she's saying. If you were to find yourself in a situation in which you were listening to someone who suddenly started to speak "through her hand," would you conclude that she was lying? Human nature is such that we seldom instinctively consider a "what else" possibility. The overwhelming majority of people would read such a gesture as an indication that she was lying, unsure, or attempting to cover something up. Perhaps that would really be the case . . . or maybe she recently had dental work or realized she had bad breath. So be sure to consider other possibilities as well.

STAY TUNED IN

Many students of body language complain, on occasion, that they find themselves tuning out for periods of time and becoming completely blind to the messages people are sending them nonverbally. You'll most likely encounter the same problem during your studies. Take heart: The art of full-time seeing and reading nonverbal communication is similar to learning a foreign language. Most language instructors strongly recommend that students spend time listening and looking at others who speak the language fluently—in other words, learning by osmosis. You don't have to constantly define what you are seeing; simply take it in. At other times, make a conscious effort to interpret gestures.

As mentioned before, we recommend that you spend time watching and "listening" in places where you'll find a lot of people, such as the airport, park, shopping malls, parties, and so on. Business gatherings that allow free expression of opinions are especially good places to practice and improve your nonverbal recognition skills. However, another great way to hone your skills is by watching reality television, roundtable discussions, debate shows, or even fictional crime shows in which the actors portray a wide range of feelings and intentions. Interview programs are also worthwhile when you consciously tune in to how the interviewee responds nonverbally to questions from the interviewer, as well as from callers.

When you watch these programs, keep a pencil and paper handy and make notes of facial expressions, gestures, and postures. Later on, using your notes, make your overall assessment of the various players. Don't forget to look for and read gesture clusters that will cement your assessment of each individual.

BE AWARE OF REACTIONS TO NONVERBAL MESSAGES

Sigmund Freud wrote, "The unconscious of one human being can react upon that of another without passing through the conscious." This means that you may subconsciously pass judgment on someone else, basing your judgment not on facts, but on intuition—in other words, on that person's body language.

A Harvard University study conducted by psychology professors Robert Rosenthal and Nalini Ambady underscored the power of nonverbal messages. The two researchers presented undergraduate students with thirty-second video clips of different teachers in classroom settings, and asked them to evaluate the teachers. The sound in the films was either scrambled or removed so that the students were judging body language only. Three quarters of the time, these evaluations matched those of students who had filled out end-of-semester evaluations after actually taking courses with the teachers. Although the latter students attributed their ratings to the teachers' friendliness or clarity, the study demonstrated that the majority of students were basing their reactions on nonverbal communication.

Using logic and thoughtful evaluation, you have the ability to avoid reacting solely to gestures and body movements. Keep in mind that body language can be deceiving if careful thought is not given to the possible cause. For example, a judge of our acquaintance had suffered a stroke that left him with a facial tic. His blinking made the attorneys appearing before him uncomfortable and nervous. Had they known or paid close enough attention to realize this wasn't voluntary, their discomfort would have been diffused.

To avoid miscommunication and misinformed reactions, it is also important to keep in mind how *your* expressions and gestures may be perceived. Whenever possible, pay attention to the nonverbal messages you are sending. Are your arms crossed? Are you leaning away? If you adopt a more open posture, perhaps others would be more receptive to what you have to say. Also be aware of your listener's body language. If you perceive that he doubts you or that he has become defensive, you have the opportunity to change your approach for better reception. Public speakers refer to this as "audience awareness" and are acutely sensitive to it. When they observe negative nonverbal messages from an audience, they quickly change the subject or come up with a joke or humorous comment to get the audience to laugh and relax.

YOUR OBSERVATION CHECKLIST

When you are learning how to read a person like a book, there is a lot to be aware of, from the head down to the feet. You will need to take it all in to get an accurate description of what someone is thinking or feeling. Be mindful of the following:

❑ Facial expressions, including the forehead, eyebrows, eyes, nose, mouth, chin, and jaw.

❑ Position of the head.

❑ Position of the back and shoulders.

❑ Arm and hand movements.

❑ Leg and foot movements, including how someone walks.

❑ Changes in tone of voice and other sounds, such as clearing the throat.

❑ Variations of all of the above as interaction progresses.

When strung together, all of these factors will form a cohesive message that will help you determine your next move in an encounter, whether it is casual, personal, or professional. This information can give you the upper hand in a situation, or at least the ability to keep the encounter flowing harmoniously and productively.

CONCLUSION

In this chapter, you learned how to set the stage for careful observation. But you cannot determine if your practice of reading people is successful until you begin acting on your perceptions, in much the way that new cars are subjected to testing before they arrive on a showroom floor, but cannot truly be evaluated until they are exposed to real-life situations. Before you start your real-world testing, though, there is much to learn. In the upcoming chapters, we will discuss the meanings of a myriad of expressions, gestures, and postures.

2

It Was Written All Over His Face

"The eyes of men converse as much as their tongues, with the advantage that the ocular dialect needs no dictionary, but is understood all the world over."

—Ralph Waldo Emerson

Perhaps the least controversial of all the areas of nonverbal communication is facial expressions. We focus our eyes on the face more than any other part of the body, and the expressions we see are widely accepted as having meaning. Virtually every one of us has encountered "a look that could kill," "a fish eye," or "a come-hither look." Facial expressions convey a wide range of emotions. A person's face is capable of nonverbally communicating many thoughts and feelings, consciously or unconsciously. In this chapter, we'll study the individual expressions of the face. Remember, however, that although we're focusing on individual expressions, you must string all the expressions together—along with gestures, postures, and words—to understand the full meaning.

STUDYING FACIAL EXPRESSIONS

People generally believe that facial expressions are very important in communicating thoughts, feelings, and emotions. However, few people know how to break down the facial expression into individual words. When shown an illustration of two groups seated across from each other at a conference table (see Figure 2.1), most people will observe that the two groups dislike each other. However, that's a

Unhappy Conference Attendees.

Figure 2.1. Opposing Sides at a Conference Table.

very general observation. If observation become deeper, the viewer will become more perceptive and begin to notice such things as a wrinkled forehead, raised eyebrows, exaggerated opening of the eyes, flaring nostrils, pursed lips, and so on. What do you see in Figure 2.1? Jot down all your observations. You will most likely have a long list. In the balance of this chapter, we'll look at how the various features of the face change depending on what's going on inside the individual's mind.

THE EYES

It's been said that the eyes are the windows to the soul. In that case, the eyelids are shades, and the eyebrows and forehead are window dressings, all of which help make a more complete picture of what's going on in someone's mind. In this section, we'll take a close look at what the eyes have to say, covering such things as eye contact, pupil dilation, blink rate, and so on. Later, we'll take a look at the complementary role the eyebrows play in the nonverbal messages communicated by the eyes.

Pleased Conference Attendees.

Eye Contact

Have you ever been listening to someone, focusing on him attentively, only to notice that as he talked, he was looking at something other than you? Have you ever been in the middle of a story and glanced up to notice that the person to whom you were speaking was watching you closely the entire time? That's because people tend to have greater eye contact when listening than when speaking. When we're paying close attention to what a person is saying, we are more likely to look at him as he talks, particularly at his eyes. This not only helps us to better understand what is being said, but also serves as a clear indicator to the person to whom we are listening that we are invested in the conversation. When we're talking, however, we're more likely to glance around or to stare at nothing in order to better visualize what we're describing.

It's often assumed that if someone does not look us in the eyes, he is either not listening or is attempting to hide something. In *The Psychology of Interpersonal Behaviour*, Michael Argyle observes that people make eye contact with each other between 30 and 60 percent of the time.

Argyle also notes that when two people's eye contact exceeds that range, they are likely either in love or getting ready to fight. If, during your people-watching exercises, you see two people looking into each other's eyes intently, you can start by making these two assumptions. But to really determine what's going on between them, you need to carefully observe their gesture clusters.

Your culture and where you live determines what you consider to be the appropriate level of eye contact in a given circumstance. In North America, people generally prefer a lot of eye contact, whereas in other countries, it's seen as an attempt at being dominant and is considered rude. Some cultures consider it inappropriate for women to make eye contact with men who are not related to them, and in other cultures, a woman making eye contact is an indication that she is a prostitute. So before you interpret a person's eye contact in a negative light, consider where that person is coming from and the reasons why he may be less inclined to make eye contact.

Another factor to take into account when observing eye contact patterns is a person's personality. A more outgoing person will generally have no problems with eye contact, whereas a more timid person may make less eye contact. It is easy to interpret a shy person's inconsistent eye contact as insincerity or an indication that he is lying, so try not to fall prey to this common mistake.

If a person is asked questions that make him uncomfortable or uncertain of how to answer, he will tend to avert his gaze. In cases where a statement or question makes him angry or defensive, he will generally have a higher amount of eye contact than usual.

When a person is gazing or staring, his eyes become still and look at one particular thing. Usually, our eyes dart around the room, taking inventory of our surroundings; this is something we're not even aware of doing, as it happens involuntarily. When our eyes rest on a particular object or person longer than they normally would, it indicates an interest in that object or person. When observing a stare or a gaze, it's important to note whether the person's eyes are focused or glazed over. If an individual is focused on the thing he is looking at, his eyes will be alert. This means that he's thinking about or analyzing the object. If a person has a distant look in his eyes and doesn't seem mentally present, chances are he's daydreaming and isn't aware of what is in front of him.

Eye Direction

During a conversation, a person's eyes will move in many directions. These directions can help you determine what's really going on inside the individual's head.

When a person looks up, she is very likely thinking or trying to remember something. This could be because she is a visual thinker and is trying to form an image in her head. Looking down can be a signal of submission, or can indicate that a person feels guilty about something. If an individual is looking to the side, be aware that she is probably annoyed. It can also be interpreted as an attempt to escape a conversation or to look at a distraction.

Pupil Dilation and Contraction

The contraction or dilation of pupils is a physiological response over which a person has no control. When you are physically close to someone, you are able to observe this dilation or contraction rather easily, especially in people with green, blue, or hazel eyes. Naturally, this physiological response often occurs as a result of the lighting; the darker it is, the more dilated the pupils will be, and vice versa. However, dilation and contraction also occur in response to one's emotions. Dilation may occur during times of arousal—that is, when someone is attracted to someone or something, the pupils may dilate. (See Figure 2.2.) Contraction may occur when someone is angry or dubious and gives you that "laser look." (See Figure 2.3.)

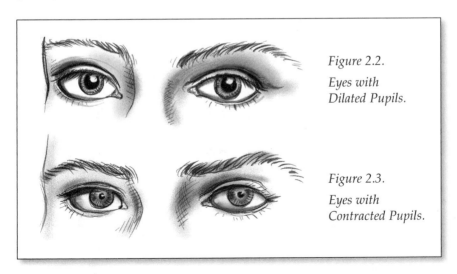

Figure 2.2.
Eyes with
Dilated Pupils.

Figure 2.3.
Eyes with
Contracted Pupils.

Blink Rate

Blinking is both a voluntary and involuntary reaction. Dry or watery eyes aside, it's important to be aware of the rate at which a person blinks. Pay attention to the blink rate of people you are talking with to get a feel for "normal" blinking, reduced blinking, and rapid blinking. Notice how things you say and do affect the rate. Do this for quite some time before you add this to the mix when trying to judge someone's intentions.

It is generally accepted that if someone is lying, she will blink more rapidly than normal. For example, a United States customs inspector always asks travelers returning to their country of origin if they have anything to declare. This seems like a silly question since the traveler has already filled out a declaration form. However, when the inspector asks the question, she looks the traveler in the eye to determine her blink rate. If the traveler blinks rapidly, she will likely have to undergo an inspection of her luggage. Moreover, law-enforcement officers take note of a suspect's blink rate to help determine guilt or innocence. Once again, a rapid blink rate may indicate guilt. On the other hand, a slow blink rate may mean that the person is intent on processing what is being said or, conversely, that she is simply not paying attention. That is why it is vital to note *all* of an individual's expressions and gestures.

Eyelid Movement

Eyelids are often overlooked in discussions about eye contact, but a little thing such as how much the whites of your eyes are showing can actually communicate more than you would think. Drooping eyelids, for example, can mean several things, so use the situation to best decide whether the person is tired, bored, depressed, lazy, or flirting. (See Figure 2.4.) Wide-open eyes usually mean that a person is interested and paying attention, although if the eyes are too wide-open, the individual is probably either surprised or afraid. (See Figure 2.5.) When not caused by a bright light, squinting indicates that the person either is evaluating what is being said or is uncertain. (See Figure 2.6.) When paired with a broad smile, squinting can also be a sign that a person feels joyful and merry.

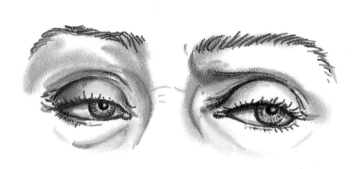

Figure 2.4. Drooping Eyelids.

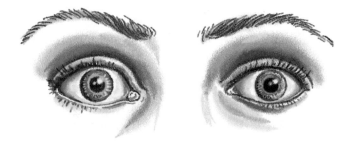

Figure 2.5. Wide-Open Eyes.

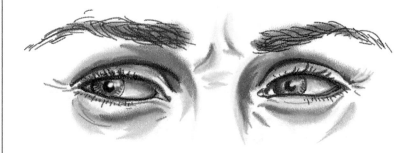

Figure 2.6. Squinting Eyes.

Figure 2.7. Raising One Eyebrow.

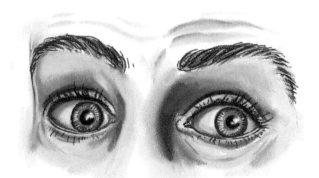

Figure 2.8. Raising Both Eyebrows.

Figure 2.9. Furrowed Eyebrows.

EYEBROWS

The eyebrows are very expressive and can be used to convey many different emotions. Some people, for instance, can raise one eyebrow. When someone arches one eyebrow only, it is usually deliberate and is a way of expressing disbelief as if he's saying, "Really? Are you sure you mean that?" (See Figure 2.7.) The rest of us are slightly more limited in how we can use our eyebrows, but we still manage to convey a range of emotions with them. For example, two raised eyebrows (see Figure 2.8) can be a sign of surprise, and are sometimes used to show that a question is being asked. When a person's eyebrows are furrowed—pulled together in the middle to form a furrow, or wrinkle—this can indicate deep concentration, anxiety, anger, or frustration. (See Figure 2.9.)

THE NOSE

Although you may not regard the nose as being especially expressive, even this feature (see Figure 2.10) has much to communicate. If a person flares her nostrils, for example, prepare yourself for a fight. (See Figure 2.11.) The widening of the nostrils is the body's way of taking in more oxygen to ready itself for a confrontation. A wrinkled nose generally indicates disgust—anything from mild disapproval to a feeling of revulsion. (See Figure 2.12.) It's as if the person has smelled something really awful. Generally, wrinkling of the nose signifies disgust with something external, such as a statement that another person has made, but it can also mean that the individual is pondering something and is not satisfied with her own ideas.

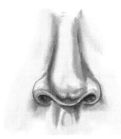 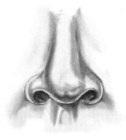 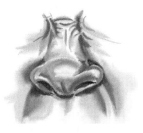

Figure 2.10.	*Figure 2.11.*	*Figure 2.12.*
Normal Nose Position.	*Flaring Nostrils.*	*Wrinkling of the Nose.*

THE MOUTH

The mouth is the only part of the body that can communicate both verbally and nonverbally. As you know, the verbal messages that come out of someone's mouth may not reflect her true thoughts or feelings. However, the nonverbal messages communicated by the mouth are rarely misleading. For example, it is fairly easy to see the difference between an authentic smile and a nervous or insincere smile. Let's take a look at what the mouth has to say when it is not engaged in verbal communication.

Smiles

There are many types of smiles. Of the sincere smiles, the three most common are the simple smile, the upper smile, and the broad smile. The simple smile, performed with closed lips, is flashed primarily by someone to acknowledge to those around him that he is well and/or pleased by a situation. (See Figure 2.13.) In the upper smile, the top incisors are exposed, and eye contact usually occurs between the individuals. (See Figure 2.14.) This smile is quite often used as a greeting between friends, family members, and well-liked coworkers or business acquaintances. A broad smile is commonly seen during, and associated with, happiness and joy. In the broad smile, both the upper and

Figure 2.13. The Simple Smile.

Figure 2.14. The Upper Smile.

Smiling Eyes

An authentic smile, technically called a Duchenne smile after French physician Guillaume Duchenne, can be distinguished from a false smile, a non-Duchenne smile, by the crinkles around the eyes. When a person has "smiling eyes," she is most likely sincere. Both Duchenne and non-Duchenne smiles involve the corners of the mouth turning up, but it is close to impossible to simulate the eye crinkles of a genuine smile.

lower incisors are exposed. (See Figure 2.15.) Eye contact rarely occurs simply because during this smile, the head is often tilted backward.

Smiles do not always indicate well-being or good intentions, however. Several decades ago, Ewan Grant of the psychology department at Birmingham University coined the term "oblong smile" for the expression people tend to use when they feel they must be polite, but are not experiencing the lightheartedness and joy that accompanies a sincere smile. In this expression, the lips are drawn back from both the upper and lower teeth, creating an oblong shape. This is not a genuine smile and could actually be referred to as a grimace. (See Figure 2.16.)

Figure 2.15. The Broad Smile.

Figure 2.16.
The Insincere Oblong Smile.

Pouts and Pursed Lips

The pout—the deliberate protrusion of the lower lip (see Figure 2.17)—can indicate many emotions. Often, the pout is used to show displeasure, disappointment, or frustration, but this same expression can also reveal sexual interest. The pout can be employed either teasingly or in earnest, but is usually intended to gently express displeasure instead of overreacting with anger. It is also an expression that is associated with being childish, however, so use it with caution, as many people become irritated when witnessing a pout.

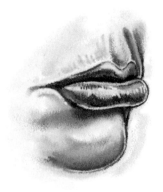

Figure 2.17. Pouting Lips.

Pursed lips are usually a sign that a person is angry. There are actually a couple of different lip positions that are considered "pursed." In one, the upper and lower lips are pressed together in controlled anger. (See Figure 2.18.) In another, the lips are squeezed together from all sides, making the mouth seem smaller and filled with tension. Either position shows that the person is trying to suppress his annoyance or attempting to refrain from comment. When the corners of his mouth are turned down into a frown, he is indicating that he is either sad or displeased.

*Figure 2.18.
Pursed Lips.*

Licking or Biting the Lips

Licking the lips is generally seen as a provocative, sexual signal. (See Figure 2.19.) If you're flirting with a guy and he licks his lips, either intentionally or unconsciously, chances are the thought of kissing you has crossed his mind. Of course, lip licking doesn't always have a sexual connotation. People routinely moisten their lips simply because they have become too dry.

Figure 2.19.
Licking the Lips.

When a person bites his lips, it is usually a sign that he's anxious, uncomfortable, frustrated, or embarrassed. (See Figure 2.20.) Lip biting can also indicate that the person is lost in thought. Although this gesture is viewed as a sign of insecurity and sometimes childishness, many people habitually bite their lips and don't even realize they're doing it.

Figure 2.20.
Biting the Lips.

THE JAW AND CHIN

While the jaw and chin may seem like stagnant facial features, they do provide some insight into a person's thoughts and feelings. For instance, tightening of the jaw muscles is much like making a fist with the face, and indicates "controlled" anger. Clenching the teeth is also a sign that someone is trying to stay in control despite feelings of resentment or irritation. Although the mouth remains closed, this activity is evidenced by the tight and/or flexing upper jaw muscles.

Jutting out one's chin, such as a small child would do when disregarding her parents' advice, indicates defiance.

MICROEXPRESSIONS

Paul Ekman—perhaps one of the foremost researchers on nonverbal behavior—has written many books on facial expressions. In his early work, Ekman was primarily concerned with what factors trigger emotion, how the face signals feelings to others, how we can learn to distinguish one reaction from another, and whether we can truly learn to control our responses. Since that early work, much research has gone into these areas, the most interesting of which is the study of microexpressions.

For the most part, people who practice control, such as poker players, negotiators, and con artists, are capable of masking their true emotions and intentions, at least on the surface. (See the inset "The Poker Face," below.) If not consciously controlled, most expressions remain

The Poker Face

A poker face is often described as an expressionless face. It gives nothing away, good, bad, or neutral. Successful poker players are often adept at keeping their feelings to themselves by controlling their body language, especially their facial expressions. Quite often, you will see these players wearing dark glasses to reduce the possibility that their eyes will give them away. Sometimes a player will adopt a false expression or mannerism in an attempt to confuse or mislead the other players with reverse psychology. This sort of behavior isn't relegated to gamblers, by the way; anyone can try to use reverse psychology by presenting contradictory expressions or maintaining a poker face.

Facial Expression and Sign Language

In this chapter, you have learned that facial expression can support, modify, or even contradict what an individual is intentionally communicating through words. Did you know that in sign language, facial expressions are also important, and help define what is being conveyed by the hands?

For example, if a person is making a declarative statement that "Grandfather is sick," using three signs in signed English or two signs in American sign language, the meaning is clear without accompanying facial gestures. If, however, someone is asking, "Grandfather is sick?" the same signs would be used, but facial, hand, and body movements would be altered to prompt an answer to the question. What if the individual did not believe that Grandfather was really sick? The same signs would be employed, but in a different configuration, and a distinct facial expression would be needed to convey the person's skepticism. So whether your companion is communicating to you in spoken words or sign language, you'll want to observe the total gesture cluster, for only then will you know what she really means.

on the face for a minimum of a few seconds and are readily detectable. Microexpressions—shorter versions of the facial expressions you've been learning about in this chapter—flash for only a brief instant and are essentially involuntary. They most often occur when someone is trying to hide his true feelings. With today's computer technology, it is possible to instantly start and stop a video recording to study the various microexpressions a person uses during conversation or questioning. But you don't need a computer to detect microexpressions if you train yourself to be aware of them. When studying a person's face in an effort to understand him better, do not discount the very brief flashes of emotion that arise. These may be more significant than the emotions that he voluntarily expresses.

CONCLUSION

Now that you are familiar with what various facial expressions may be telling you, you need to combine what the face reveals with what the rest of the body has to say. Many people talk with their hands and arms, and even with their shoulders as an extension of their arms. What they do with their legs and feet—how they stand and walk, for instance—adds to the mix of body language. In the next chapter, we'll take a close look at what the rest of the body is communicating.

When Facial Expressions Lie

The face is a dual system that includes expressions which are deliberately chosen, as well as those that occur spontaneously, often without the person even being aware of what her face is saying. The parts of the face that are the most revealing of *true* feelings—not necessarily the emotions that the person wants to convey—are the eyes, eyebrows, and mouth.

The blink rate of the eyes is indicative of comfort levels. The faster the blink rate, the more likely it is that a person is lying, unsure, or uncomfortable. Make yourself aware of a speaker's resting blink rate, because it differs from person to person. Notice how often the eyebrows rise every time she says the words, "how," "when," "why," and "where." This is a key factor in determining someone's level of sincerity. Finally, pay attention to the individual's lips and mouth while she listens. If the mouth twitches, tightens, or puckers, she is giving you a clear indication that she disagrees with you—regardless of her overall facial expression.

3

Talking With the Hands and Other Parts of the Body

"Tis the sublime of man . . . to know ourselves parts
and proportions of one wondrous whole."

—Samuel Taylor Coleridge, *Religious Musings*

he rest of the body has as much to say as the face. In this chapter, we'll look at the individual meanings of hand and arm gestures, as well as how the way we walk can communicate important information about mood and intention. Body movements are usually more obvious than facial expressions, and because they can be observed more readily from a distance, you can read a person like a book from across the room—or even across the street—if the need arises. Since the hands tend to be the most animated part of the body aside from the face, this chapter begins there.

THE HANDS

Our hands are some of the most useful tools we possess. What a person does with his hands can reveal quite a bit about what he is thinking or feeling—and, in the case of sign language, can convey as much as the spoken word! This section begins with one of the most common hand gestures that people often use to evaluate one another: the handshake. Then we'll discuss other hand gestures, as well as the meaning of touching.

The Handshake

The modern handshake is a modification of an ancient gesture in which people raised both hands when they met to show that they were free of weapons. During the time of the Roman Empire, men grasped each other at the forearm. Today, we place our hands palm to palm as a gesture of welcome. The handshake signifies openness and union.

A firm, dry handshake is generally regarded as an indication that someone is confident and in control, whereas a weak handshake may be seen as signaling a "weak" personality, and a sweaty palm may be interpreted as a sign of nervousness. However, all of these assumptions are generalizations. A man with great strength may not grip another man's hand tightly in fear of accidentally causing pain, while an artist or surgeon who relies on her hands for her work may not grip tightly in an effort to protect herself. Likewise, someone with arthritis may choose not to shake hands at all. Sweaty palms may simply indicate that a person is overheated.

The standard or equal handshake is one in which both palms are vertical and the pressure is about the same on both sides. (See Figure 3.1.) In an equal handshake, the hands are gripped in a firm, but not crushing, hold. Both parties maintain eye contact as they pump the hands no more than three times. This handshake shows confidence, but not arrogance. In order to further convey a friendly, sincere attitude, it is important to smile.

Figure 3.1. The Standard or Equal Handshake.

In the "politician's handshake," one of the people involved uses two hands instead of one. (See Figure 3.2.) When the right hand is grasped, the left hand cradles the handshake. An alternative to the cradling is placing one's hand on the other person's forearm or shoulder. Such a handshake generally implies sincerity and genuine interest in the other person. This cradling handshake is not unusual when

Figure 3.2. The Politician's Handshake.

two very old and dear friends meet after being separated for a long time. In such instances, a "bear hug" may follow the handshake. However, most of us feel uncomfortable when someone we don't know very well greets us in such a manner. And whenever they do, we have a tendency to view the greeting as being insincere.

When expressing sincere feelings during a crisis, people rarely shake hands. Instead, they gently hold the other person's hands in theirs and use congruous facial expressions to communicate their deep empathy. (See Figure 3.3.) An embrace often accompanies the sentimental words. This is a way of showing the person in need that you are there for her and that you sympathize with her situation.

Figure 3.3.

Sympathetic Hand Holding.

In some cases, a person may unconsciously display feelings of superiority in an initial handshake. This involves extending the hand with the palm facing downward so that the other person is forced to turn his palm up in a submissive manner. (See Figure 3.4.) Conversely, someone who is unconsciously displaying feelings of inferiority will offer his hand for a shake with his palm facing upward, rather than aligning it with the other vertically outstretched palm. (See Figure 3.5.) Another variation in which one person's hand ends up on top and the

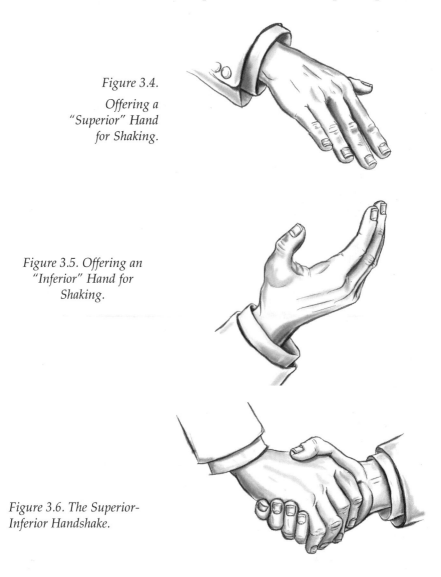

Figure 3.4.

Offering a "Superior" Hand for Shaking.

Figure 3.5. Offering an "Inferior" Hand for Shaking.

Figure 3.6. The Superior-Inferior Handshake.

other person's hand is on the bottom involves a mid-shake switch. A person will extend his hand and, grabbing hold of the other person's hand, will turn his hand so that the other individual's palm is directly below his. This is a simple nonverbal greeting that says, "I've got the upper hand." (See Figure 3.6.)

It is important to be aware of cultural differences in handshakes. For example, the French shake hands when entering and leaving a room, and the Germans have a custom of pumping the hand just once, instead of two or more shakes. When traveling, it's a good idea to learn the proper method of greeting in order to avoid missteps.

Hand Signals

Earlier in the chapter, you learned how even the simple act of shaking hands can unconsciously reveal a great deal about your emotions and intentions. The same is true of finger pointing and other hand positions. But, of course, we also use *conscious* and *deliberate* hand signals to communicate emotions and ideas. For instance, in our culture, a crossing of the index and middle finger of either hand is commonly used to indicate a wish for good luck. Another familiar gesture is the "okay" sign in which the index finger and thumb are brought together to form a circle, while the three remaining fingers are held apart, slightly bent. As its name implies, this is a positive gesture showing that everything is going well. The classic thumbs-up sign is another positive gesture used to indicate that the situation is good, that victory is yours, or that you *hope* that things will turn out well.

When discussing hand signals in the United States, it seems only right to talk a little bit about William Ellsworth Hoy. An outfielder for five major league baseball teams in the late 1800s, Hoy made history as the first deaf player in the major leagues, and is also credited with creating the hand signals that are still used in baseball today. Unable to hear the call of an umpire when an opposing player was at bat, Hoy asked his third-base coach to raise his left arm to indicate a ball, and his right arm to signal that a strike was called. Gradually, other hand signals came into common use to accommodate the special needs of this player, and it was found that these gestures were useful to the other members of the team, as well. Now, umpires, coaches, and players alike rely on hand signals for vital communication during games.

Open Palms

Open palms indicate openness and sincerity. (See Figure 3.7.) Small children often display their palms when they are proud of something they've accomplished. (Those same hands will find their way behind the back when kids feel guilty or uncertain about something.) One out-stretched palm indicates that something is expected, whether it be money, an object, or an idea.

Figure 3.7.

The Open-Hands Gesture of Sincerity.

Figure 3.8.

Clenched, Interlocked Hands.

Fists, Wringing Hands, and Clenched Hands

Imagine a person who is sitting in a meeting with her hands tightly clenched, saying, "I have an open mind and sincerely want to settle." Surely, her counterpart would consciously or unconsciously see the incongruity between the verbal and nonverbal signals. While open palms indicate openness and sincerity, clenched fists indicate the opposite. This deceptive approach to getting what one wants would likely backfire and cause hostility and aggression between the parties.

When someone is under stress, such as when that person is feeling defensive, she may clench her hands together, with fingers tightly interlaced. (See Figure 3.8.) Clenched hands show that a person is try-ing to suppress strong emotions, usually anger.

A clenched fist is sometimes used to emphasize what is being said and may be employed during a motivational speech. Some people openly clench their fists and wave them in the air to make a point or to express strong emotions, such as serious opposition. Others stick their clenched fists under their arms or in their pockets to hide what they are feeling. (See Figure 3.9.) In *The Expression of the Emotions in Man and Animals*, Charles Darwin noted that a clenched fist signifies determination, anger, and possible hostile action. He also observed that this gesture may cause the other person to clench his fists as well, which could escalate into a heated argument or fight.

Figure 3.9.

Crossed Arms with Clenched Fists.

Figure 3.10.

Wringing the Hands.

If a person is twisting and squeezing her hands together (see Figure 3.10)—in other words, wringing her hands—she is probably anxious. This motion is a cousin of the clenched fist. Someone who is being questioned about serious issues, or who is required to account for her actions, will often use this nervous gesture, provided, of course, that she has something to be nervous about.

If you are interacting with someone who is clenching or wringing her hands, give her something to read, or do something that will force her to unlock her hands. You will likely notice a softening of her attitude, which will give you an opportunity to make the most of the situation.

Steepling the Hands

Steepling is a gesture in which a person, with fingers pointing upwards, touches the fingertips of both hands together. (See Figure 3.11.) This gesture is occasionally misinterpreted as something other than a display of confidence, which is what it usually is. For people in the know, this gesture can be defined as someone who is "sitting in the catbird seat," an idiom implying that the individual has the upper hand. When this gesture is accompanied by a slight upward curling of the lips—a sly smile—you know the person feels like "the cat who swallowed the canary" and got away with it. (See the inset "Hank Meets the King of Cool" on page 37 for an interesting anecdote about the steepling gesture.)

Most of the time, a person uses the steeple unconsciously. However, it may also be used consciously to communicate great security and self-confidence. For example, a business executive was advised to use the gesture when he had made his final offer in a negotiation. As instructed, the executive stated the offer, sat back in his chair, smiled, and steepled his fingers. His client took a long time in answering, looking frequently at the executive before finally saying, "You got a deal!" The gesture worked like a charm.

Figure 3.11.
Steepling the Hands.

Hank Meets the King of Cool

Steve McQueen was an American movie actor who was dubbed the "King of Cool." He appeared in many popular films, including the classic *The Great Escape*. Many years back, coauthor Hank had a most interesting experience when he was flying first class and found himself seated beside McQueen. They began to talk, and Hank expressed his feeling that McQueen's portrayal of a poker player in *The Cincinnati Kid* was not very convincing.

The King of Cool crossed his arms and glared at Hank with his piercing blue eyes and said, "What the hell do you mean?"

Hank explained that in one important scene in which McQueen's character held a winning hand against his opponent, McQueen used the steepling gesture after placing his bet. Hank further explained that no self-respecting professional would ever display such a gesture, unless he was bluffing. McQueen's character was certainly not bluffing; it was a nonverbal mistake on the part of the actor.

McQueen quickly uncrossed his arms and snapped his fingers, as if a light bulb had just gone off. He told Hank that others had made similar comments about his portrayal but couldn't give a reason for their dubiousness other than that they just "sensed it."

Then, McQueen shook Hank's hand to thank him for the information. The rest of the flight proceeded without confrontation and was a pleasure, one that Hank always recalls fondly.

Pointing

Finger pointing is a common gesture used to "drive home a point" or seriously emphasize something. However, once you consciously avoid using this gesture, you'll be amazed by how well you are still able to communicate your thoughts and ideas. Why avoid it? The answer is simple: It is a defense-provoking gesture. Coupled with a raised voice, finger pointing can lead to a serious argument. In fact, finger pointing is quite common during arguments and heated discussions. If, however, the tone of voice indicates self-control and restraint, some finger pointing generally doesn't create as much defensiveness.

Politicians and clergymen who use "condemning" finger pointing generally don't arouse defensiveness in their audience simply because no one in the group thinks the gesture is meant specifically for him. In a one-on-one situation, however, there is no doubt as to the individual for whom the gesture is intended, and it can cause some problems.

Touching

Touching something or someone is a sign of pride, ownership, or perceived rights. It is also a gesture of interest, concern, love, understanding, empathy, assurance, or reassurance. Very strong aspects of a love relationship are fundamentally based on touching. To determine the intentions behind someone's touch, as with most messages having to do with body language, you must take in the full picture to better understand what a touch signifies.

THE ARMS AND SHOULDERS

Our arms are very expressive. They can convey a huge amount of information very effectively. You can easily tell how comfortable a person is in any given situation by noting the size of his arm movements. The less comfortable he is, the smaller the movements. Similarly, large, elaborate arm movements indicate that the speaker is fully committed to what he is saying.

Crossing the arms over the chest as a sign of defensiveness is very common throughout the world. (See Figure 3.12.) Women tend to fold their arms considerably lower on the body, as shown in Figure 3.13. Crossed arms accompanied by clenched fists reinforce defensiveness. (See Figure 3.9.)

Figure 3.12.
A Man's
Crossed Arms.

Figure 3.13.
A Woman's
Crossed Arms.

Figure 3.14.

Relaxed, Straight Shoulders.

Figure 3.15.

Slumped Shoulders.

The shoulders are more limited in their movements than the arms, but information can still be gleaned from them if you pay attention. When shoulders are held low and straight, without tension, they indicate that the individual is relaxed and self-confident. (See Figure 3.14.) On the other hand, shoulders that are slumped forward, possibly with a bowed head, suggest that the person is defeated, unhappy, or perhaps simply fatigued. (See Figure 3.15.) The classic shrugging (raising and lowering) of the shoulders means, "I don't know." (See Figure 3.16.) Sometimes, this is accompanied by raised eyebrows.

Figure 3.16.

Shrugging Shoulders.

WALKING

A great deal can be learned by watching an individual's legs and feet. In fact, the language of the legs is more reliable than that of any other part of the body because people usually don't think about their legs when they're trying to mask how they feel. In the next chapter, you will learn how sitting and standing positions can clearly communicate our thoughts and emotions. The remainder of this chapter will focus on one of the most important (and revealing) things we do with our legs—walking.

The way we walk is almost as unique as our fingerprints. Because of the distinctive way each of us walks, we are often recognizable from a distance by people who are familiar with us. Yet our manner of walking can change depending on how we feel at the moment, and can also change as we age.

Generally, people who walk rapidly and swing their arms freely tend to be goal-oriented and in pursuit of something, whereas people who habitually walk with their hands in their pockets, regardless of the weather, tend to be critical and secretive. Someone who feels dejected may also walk with his hands in his pockets, but this will usually be accompanied by a shuffling step and a lowered head. This person will seldom look up to take notice of where he is headed. (See Figure 3.17.) A person who walks rapidly with both hands on his hips is usually in a hurry to reach his goal in the shortest time possible. (See Figure 3.18.) Someone who is in the process of making a major decision has a slow pace and may clasp his hands behind his back, pausing occasionally

You're Out!

No baseball fan would be surprised to see an umpire cross his arms over his chest if a call were contested by a coach or manager—as long as the umpire wasn't wearing a chest protector. In that case, an umpire would tend to place both hands on his hips and jut his chin toward those who disputed his decision. Furthermore, if an umpire believed he had heard enough, he would either point to the dugout, which is a nonverbal signal meaning "You're out of the game!" or simply turn his back and walk away.

Figure 3.17.

The Dejected Walker.

Figure 3.18.

The Goal-Oriented Walker.

Figure 3.19.

The Preoccupied Walker.

Figure 3.20.

The Strutter.

to think. (See Figure 3.19.) An individual who is self-satisfied and, perhaps, arrogant is likely to hold his head high and exaggerate the swinging motion of his arms, strutting. The walking pace is deliberate and calculated to impress. (See Figure 3.20.)

"Setting the pace" is an expression that applies to leaders whose subordinates must walk rapidly to keep up with them. Keeping up is a nonverbal sign of loyalty, dedication, and commitment to the leaders' goals and objectives.

CONCLUSION

As you learned in this chapter, there's a lot that a person's body will say to you if you pay attention. Now that you have some of the vocabulary necessary to read people, you can start stringing these "words" together into sentences and paragraphs. In the next chapter, we'll discuss a range of attitudes and the gesture clusters that tend to display them.

4

What's With the Attitude?

"O, what men dare do! What men may do!
What men daily do, not knowing what they do!"

—William Shakespeare, *Much Ado About Nothing*

ecognizing the overall attitude a person displays through her words and gesture clusters is important for assessing her intentions. It is also valuable to sense subsequent changes in state of mind, whether they are positive or negative. For example, being aware that someone's open attitude has suddenly become defensive and angry can alert you to the need for a different approach.

In this chapter, we will take a look at a variety of attitudes—those that complement each other as well as those that oppose each other. Since many gestures overlap from one mind-set to another, you will note that some outlooks are also mentioned within discussions of similar or opposing attitudes. This chapter begins with the most innocuous and easily recognizable attitude of all, openness.

OPENNESS

Charles Darwin noted that when animals demonstrate submissiveness, a form of openness, they lay on their backs and expose the soft underside of their body and throats to a perceived opponent. Likewise, humans often show openness by standing with hands at waist level and their palms facing upwards. (See Figure 4.1.) In a sense, the open hands expose the person's "underbelly," and—along with a congruent facial expression—communicate a message of honesty and sincerity. Sometimes words such as "I have nothing to hide" accompany this gesture.

Darwin observed that often, even the most hostile animal does not take advantage of the one demonstrating openness. Similarly, openness in humans encourages an attitude of sincerity and frankness in those around them.

Figure 4.1.
The Open Hands of Sincerity.

DEFENSIVENESS

In contrast to the gestures that indicate openness are those that guard the body or emotions against a threatened assault. Be aware that sometimes, if openness is misunderstood or mishandled, it can become defensiveness. Of all the mannerisms, gestures, postures, and facial expressions, defensiveness indicated by the crossing of the arms tends to be the easiest to recognize and the one most likely to influence the behavior of others.

The crossed-arm gesture (see Figure 4.2) is very common in negotiations when someone is displeased with the proceedings. It is important to immediately recognize such defensiveness, figure out what motivated it, and attempt to diffuse the negative emotion. Frequently, in failed negotiations, an offer, demand, or request is unsuccessful simply because someone became defensive and it was not addressed and diffused. When this change in attitude occurs, it makes reaching a concession, agreement, or settlement much more difficult. Conducting a successful negotiation is like a journey down a river full of rapids. One has to be aware of the rapids and react accordingly; otherwise, the boat will capsize.

Another sign of defensiveness or disinterest is sitting with one leg draped over the arm of a chair. (See Figure 4.3.) While on the surface, this may simply seem like a relaxed position, a person who displays this nonverbal behavior is generally demonstrating hostility or a lack of concern for the other person's needs. Along these lines, flight attendants have reported that travelers who straddle the armrest are often demanding and difficult to please. Salespeople find that buyers who sit in a similar position during a sales call are a hard sell. This behavior can indicate a nonverbal announcement of territorial rights and power position in the transaction.

Figure 4.2.
The Defensive Crossed-Arms
Position.

Another common gesture that can indicate defensiveness is crossing the legs. (See Figure 4.4.) During the stage of a negotiation when issues are being presented and discussed, the legs are usually uncrossed. When two or more people cross their legs, it usually signals the beginning of confrontation. During periods in which the negotiators are reaching agreements, the legs are seldom crossed. This is because the participants are leaning forward not only to narrow the distance between one another, but also to narrow their relative position on the issues.

Figure 4.3.

*The Indifferent
Leg-Over-Arm-of-Chair
Position.*

Figure 4.4.

*The Defensive Crossed-Legs
Position.*

EVALUATION

Perhaps some of the most misinterpreted gestures are evaluation gestures. These gestures indicate pensiveness or thoughtfulness. As you know, much of our effectiveness in business and social life depends upon communication, knowledge, and appraisal of feedback, all of which are vital for understanding how our messages are received.

There are specific gestures that communicate that a person is evaluating what has been said, but they may be hard to discern without some awareness. For example, a young teacher is explaining a principle and takes note of a student who is staring at her; he's not blinking, his body is erect, and his feet are planted firmly on the floor. There is little or no body motion. She assumes this student is listening to every word she says. Is she correct? If your answer is yes, you're wrong. This student is a classic example of someone who is *trying* to act as if he's

May I Take Your Jacket?

In formal business meetings, when people prepare to sit down at a large conference table, they seldom take off their suit jackets, but whether or not they leave their jackets buttoned can nonverbally communicate their openness or defensiveness. When a person is feeling friendly, relaxed, and comfortable, he tends to unbutton his jacket. If his jacket is unbuttoned and someone says something he dislikes, he may button it again and cross his arms. Those whose jackets are unbuttoned tend to be the most involved in the discussion and usually lean forward with arms and elbows on the table. Those who keep their jackets buttoned and sit in a more rigid, upright position, sometimes with arms crossed, tend to be less involved.

When the attendees at a meeting start talking about matters that are common to all present and it seems as if they have reached possible agreements-in-principle, people begin taking off their jackets. This is a sign the negotiation is headed in a positive direction. Conversely, if people continue to leave their jackets on, the meeting is probably headed in a negative direction.

"all ears." The student who is truly listening intently is sitting toward the edge of his chair, upper body leaning forward, with his head slightly tilted to one side, perhaps supported by a hand. (See Figure 4.5.) A tilted head generally indicates that someone is listening carefully and

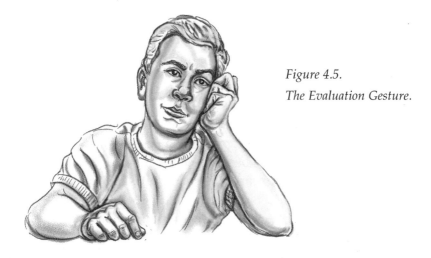

Figure 4.5.
The Evaluation Gesture.

is evaluating what is being said. It is as C.H. Woolbert wrote in "The Audience": "When a student in a classroom becomes really absorbed in the problem at hand, he is likely to slip down on his shoulder blades, spread his feet, ruffle his hair and do any number of unconventional deeds. Let the spell be broken, and he sits up, rearranges his clothes and again become socially proper."

The well-known statue "The Thinker," by Auguste Rodin, is a classic example of someone who is deep in thought and seeking the solution to a problem. This pose, or variations of it, is often used in real life and indicates that a person is evaluating something that is difficult or puzzling.

Sometimes a person will perform a critical evaluation gesture cluster, in which she brings a hand to her cheek and extends her index finger alongside her face, with her other fingers positioned below her mouth. (See Figure 4.6.) Not only is this person evaluating what is being said, she is critiquing the ideas presented.

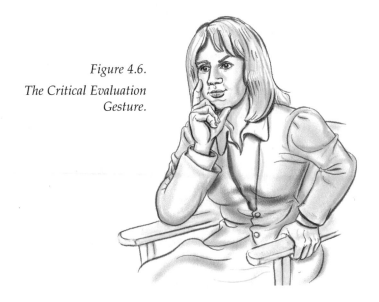

Figure 4.6.
The Critical Evaluation Gesture.

Another evaluation gesture is stroking the chin, or, in the case of bearded men, stroking the beard. (See Figure 4.7.) This "let me consider" gesture usually appears when a person is in the process of making a decision. A common facial expression associated with this gesture is slight squinting of the eyes, as if the person were trying to see a better possibility.

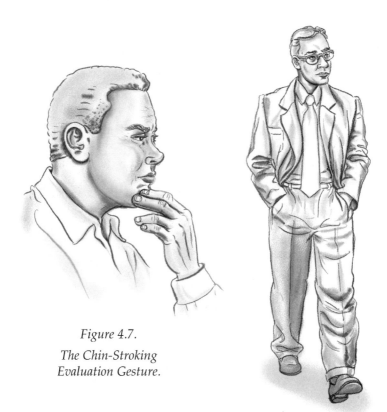

Figure 4.7.

The Chin-Stroking Evaluation Gesture.

Figure 4.8. The Pacer.

When a person gets up and begins pacing around the room, this is another strong indication that he is evaluating what has been said. Many people perform this activity because they think better on their feet. It is usually a positive gesture, so if you note someone pacing in thought, remain quiet and wait for him to speak. Don't interrupt, because it may prevent the individual from reaching a decision or making an offer. That's a classic example of how some negotiators work against their own needs because they are unable to keep quiet.

Salespeople are generally very good at reading "the pacer." (See Figure 4.8.) A skilled salesperson learns early on to wait patiently when a prospective customer is pacing, because he knows it is a sign that a decision is being made.

When a person pinches the bridge of her nose, she is often communicating great thought and concern about a decision being made. A variation of this gesture is when someone who is experiencing intense inner conflict lowers her head and pinches the nose. (See Figure 4.9.) It is almost as if she is testing whether this is reality or perhaps a bad dream. In most instances, the person also closes her eyes. This gesture may indicate serious inner doubt. For example, an attorney observed that one particular judge would use this gesture when he was uncertain if the defendant on trial was guilty or innocent. If he firmly suspected guilt, the attorney noted that this gesture would be absent from the judge's body language.

Figure 4.9.

Pinching the Bridge of the Nose.

It is a common evaluation gesture to move eyeglasses lower on the nose and peer over their rim at the person who is speaking. (See Figure 4.10.) The recipient of such a look may feel as if he is being closely scrutinized. If this happens to be one of your gestures, be aware of the negative effect it has on others and eliminate it if you do not wish to evoke this response.

Another gesture of people who wear glasses is the procrastination pause, which allows time for further thought. This occurs when the person takes off his glasses and slowly and deliberately cleans the lenses. The pause gesture may be performed in silence or while the person

Figure 4.10.
Peering Over Eyeglasses.

is speaking slowly. There are some people who have consciously mastered this gesture and often use it during periods of confrontation to quiet things down or perhaps to simply "buy time" and delay their decisions. A similar action is to remove the glasses and place the tip between or near the lips. (See Figure 4.11.) This indicates that the person is taking time to listen and evaluate what is being said.

Figure 4.11.
Buying Time to Think.

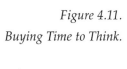

SUSPICION, UNCERTAINTY, SECRETIVENESS, AND DOUBT

All of the gestures that communicate suspicion, uncertainty, secretiveness, and doubt have a common negative message. The difference is in the importance of the information and the impact it will have on your goals or objectives. For example, a child in elementary school who is hiding something from her teacher differs greatly from an elected official who is withholding important information that could prevent a war.

The gestures which indicate that a person is being secretive or not completely forthcoming are sometimes referred to as "left-handed" gestures, because the left hand is often brought to the face. For example, during a business meeting, a colleague of ours was very reticent about stating his opposing position on an issue. He wasn't volunteering his thoughts and opinions, which left us wondering what was on his mind. Every time we approached the areas that were sensitive to him, be would bring his left hand to his mouth. Understanding this gesture, we turned our statements into questions that might help him reveal the strong emotions he was feeling. Upon answering the questions, he disclosed how vehemently he felt about our proposals. Had we not been aware of the silent messages his gesture communicated, we might have reached a decision that would have been very unwise and costly in the long run. During business meetings, there will usually be people who disagree with the proposals and decisions but, unfortunately, don't share their thoughts and feelings with the group. Worse yet, they may suggest what they think the group wants to hear instead of what they believe is the best course of action. This type of behavior works negatively in two ways: First, the people involved don't contribute what they think is important, and second, they leave the meeting feeling frustrated and angry with themselves for not stating their true ideas.

Avoiding eye contact is another sign which may reveal that someone is being secretive or insincere. When you attempt to make eye contact with a person who is not completely forthcoming, she tends to look away. Many law-enforcement officers take note of this during the questioning process. In one case, a police officer was interrogating a well-known actor who had been involved in a car accident. The officer said that whenever the actor answered his questions truthfully and completely, he would look him in the eye. However, when the actor was falsifying or withholding information, he would look away mid-sentence. The officer knew that by returning to the words the actor used when looking away, he could press for more information in an effort to reveal the truth.

Be aware, however, that many people consciously make an effort to maintain eye contact when they lie because they are aware that a lack of eye contact can give them away. In fact, some people overcompensate by making too much eye contact. If you suspect that a person is lying, watch for any abnormalities in eye contact levels, because too much eye contact may be just as good an indicator of false words as too little.

A certain amount of what we say to others may be received with doubt, suspicion, uncertainty, and/or rejection. The gesture cluster most apparent when people are harboring these feelings is the crossing of the arms and/or legs; moving away slightly; or turning sideways, exposing the shoulder rather than the front of the body, accompanied by a sideways glance. (See Figure 4.12.) (The sideways glance can be performed sitting or standing.) If the individual is wearing glasses, she may tip her head forward slightly and peer over the rim of her glasses.

Figure 4.12.
The Sideways Glance.

As the expression "giving someone a cold shoulder" implies, the sideways motion and accompanying indirect glance usually means a rejection of what has been said. It's not uncommon for these gestures to be paired with an angry question, such as, "What the heck are you talking about?

Sometimes accompanying the "cold shoulder," and sometimes used alone, is the gesture of touching the nose, which is a classic expression of doubt. (See Figure 4.13.) A person will generally touch his nose when he is not sure if he should tell you something, or when he doubts a statement that was made. (Keep in mind, however, that this gesture may also indicate suspicion, uncertainty, or defensiveness.)

Figure 4.13.
Touching the Nose in Doubt.

Many years ago, a student of the late Professor Ray L. Birdwhistell—a leading anthropologist and expert on how people communicate with body motions—was asked by the professor for his opinion of one of the professor's books. The young man said he had enjoyed the book very much, but as he made the statement, he rubbed his nose slightly.

Professor Birdwhistell smiled and said, "The truth is you didn't like it all!"

Unsure of how he had given himself away, the student admitted he'd read only a few pages and "found them all very dull." He had rubbed his nose in front of the wrong man!

During a televised interview program, a well-known news commentator was asked, "What will historians think of today's youth and their ideals?" The commentator, who likely had been trained to keep his hands away from his face, momentarily forgot and brought his right-hand index finger alongside his nose saying, "I believe historians will see today's youths as the greatest patriots this country has ever had!" Here are four different doubts the commentator may have had: 1) Whether to answer the question, 2) Whether he truly believed what he was about to say, 3) Doubt as to how to communicate his beliefs, or 4) Doubt over how his answer might affect his image with the studio and TV audience. When evaluating all his previously observed gestures and their congruity when he spoke, we reached the conclusion that it was number four—how the audience would receive his remarks.

Besides the gesture of touching the nose, two other related gestures that indicate doubt are rubbing behind or beside the ear with the index finger, and rubbing the eye. (See Figures 4.14 and 4.15.) Both gestures are very common and may be seen daily during conversations.

Figure 4.14.
Rubbing the Face in Doubt.

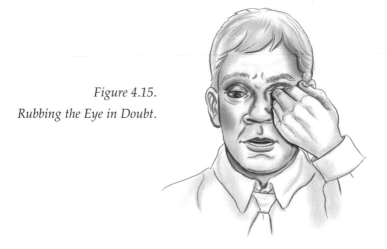

Figure 4.15.
Rubbing the Eye in Doubt.

A seminar attendee once mentioned that he put all of his offers or counteroffers "on the nose" of the person with whom he was negotiating. He further explained that the main gesture he was aware of was touching the areas of the nose, ear, or eyes. Such gestures always seemed to signify how far or near he was to a possible agreement or settlement. He found that at the beginning of a negotiation, when both parties were jockeying for position, there was a certain amount of nose touching. Then, as the negotiation proceeded toward more favorable circumstances, he saw fewer of these gestures. When he sensed that a settlement was possible, there were very few nose-, ear-, and eye-

Is Your Nose Itchy or Are You Just Doubting Me?

Always beware of interpreting any individual gesture as an absolute. Sometimes a person will rub her nose simply because it itches. Fortunately, there is a distinct difference between rubbing the nose because it itches and nonverbally communicating a negative stance. A person who is scratching her nose will do it somewhat vigorously, while a person who is doubtful or perhaps lying will use a more gentle motion. Also, a person who is doubtful or lying will usually display additional gestures such as crossing her arms and twisting her body away from you. She may also blink her eyes rapidly.

touching gestures. Moreover, people at the negotiating table were all seated with uncrossed arms and leaning toward the center of the table. They had "narrowed the distance" between the two parties.

READINESS

Some people equate readiness with aggression. Here, however, we use the word in relation to a goal-oriented achiever who, because of his great motivation, usually has little time for hostile behavior. Such people might well be what the late Dr. Abraham Maslow—often considered the father of humanistic psychology—described as "self-actualizing." (*Self-actualization* is the realization of one's full potential.) Some or all of the following gestures might fit such a person perfectly.

A classic readiness gesture is placing both hands on the hips. (See Figure 4.16.) An assertive person who is ready to take on any task may be seen standing in such a position. (While this gesture is use by both men and women, women are more likely than men to place only one

Figure 4.16.

Signaling Readiness While Standing.

hand on a hip.) This gesture is common in athletes when they are waiting to participate in an event, and is also common during a business
meeting when someone is delivering a message about which he is very
serious. (This may be followed by the crossing of the arms as he awaits
potentially negative responses from the attendees.) The hands-on-hips
gesture can also be seen in a child who is determined to do something,
with or without approval. In men, the gesture is sometimes accompanied by a hitching-up-one's-trousers movement.

A strong-willed person who is displaying the hands-on-hips gesture
may also be standing with his legs wider apart than they would normally be. This gesture cluster emphasizes his determination and commitment to what he is saying, doing, or planning to achieve. The
readiness position of a person who is seated instead of standing is similar. When looking at Figure 4.17, note the congruency of the following:
1) leaning forward, 2) the bent elbow and hand resting on the leg, and
3) legs apart as if ready to jump up and get involved in an activity.

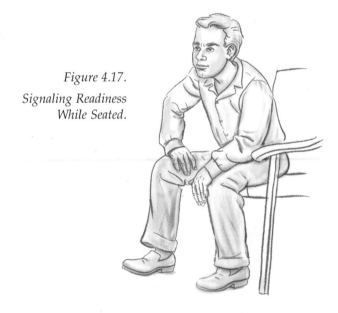

Figure 4.17.

*Signaling Readiness
While Seated.*

A person who demonstrates these readiness gestures is also interested in what is being said or done—not necessarily because he wants
to be involved, but because he is intrigued by the speaker's words.
This is perhaps where the expression "he was sitting on the edge of his
chair" originated.

In a business meeting, someone who moves toward the edge of the chair is generally getting ready to compromise, cooperate, buy, accept, or make an offer; in other words, it signifies readiness to take action. Salespeople welcome this gesture. It is their "objective achieved" sign. However, if negative gestures are involved, this position can also signal a "call it quits" attitude, and may indicate that the person is about to stand up and call off the negotiation or end the

Let's Wrap It Up ... Or Chat a While Longer

A clear indication that someone wishes to end a conversation or a meeting is the turning of his body toward the door or other point of exit. This can be true whether it's a business meeting or just an informal exchange with friends, family, or strangers. This gesture is clearly telling you that the other person would like to end the discussion and leave. If the individual happens to be seated, you'll most likely also notice that he is having a difficult time sitting still—that he has "ants in the pants." This person would dearly like to be somewhere else.

If you are faced with these gestures, you have two options. If you do not wish to end the conversation yet, ask a personal question. If you are willing to end the discussion, say something like, "I think that covers everything. Let's get back to work." Then watch how quickly the other person agrees, stands up, and leaves. Of all the gestures that people use, these are the most often overlooked. Being aware of these gestures will save you from talking to "blank walls."

During the last half hour of a social visit, people generally begin positioning their bodies to "take leave." An observant and thoughtful host will notice these gestures and end the visit by saying something like, "I'm so glad you came tonight. . . ."

Alternatively, if someone wishes to discuss an important matter with you, and hesitates to do so while you are conversing about a variety of topics, instead of positioning his body toward an exit, he will inch closer to you as if getting ready to whisper in your ear. If you notice such behavior, you can make it easier for the person to reveal his information by saying something along the lines of, "Is there something you want to tell me?" If you are correct, you'll see relief on his face as he opens up and gets the matter off his chest.

meeting. (See the inset "Let's Wrap It Up . . . Or Chat a While Longer" on page 59 to learn about signs that someone is ready to "call it quits.")

AGGRESSIVENESS

Sometimes, when someone feels aggressive towards you, he will narrow the distance between the two of you as if he wants to speak in confidence. Usually, when someone uses this subtle aggressive gesture, the normal distance of twenty-three to twenty-five inches is reduced to approximately thirteen inches, and the other individual lowers his voice to just above a whisper so that others are unable to hear what he says. The message that he wants to get closer to you and confide in you is simply a pretense. Before you take this person into your confidence, ask questions to determine his true motivation.

A more aggressive posture is the showdown gesture. In this gesture cluster, a person quickly stands up, spreads her hands on the top of the table, and verbally expresses her feelings. (See Figure 4.18.) In most instances, these feelings are hostile, defensive, and disruptive. This is a "Listen to me, damn it" gesture that may lead to serious consequences. It takes a very cool, calm, and collected person to settle things down. Should someone behave in such a manner, we strongly recommend that you don't throw any logs onto her emotional fire. Unfortunately, that is precisely what some people do in real-life situations.

Figure 4.18.
The Showdown Gesture.

When faced with aggressiveness, it is wise to use silence effectively and not react emotionally. For example, coauthors Hank and Jerry once experienced such a situation during a meeting with a publisher who became antagonistic after hearing their terms and conditions. Taking a deep breath, they exchanged glances. Without saying a word, they began putting papers in their briefcase as if getting ready to leave. Neither looked at the irate publisher when he sat back down in his chair.

As Hank and Jerry got ready to stand up, the publisher said, "Where are you going? I was only joking . . . let's negotiate!" Hank and Jerry had used silence effectively to temper the outburst, which the publisher may have been employing as a tactic. The negotiation of terms proceeded smoothly.

SHYNESS

In group situations, it is often the person who has spoken the least who has the most important things to say. If you are conducting a business meeting, be aware of the "shyness syndrome," which is seen when a person listens for long periods of time and doesn't say much, but—through her gestures and facial expressions—shows that she has many ideas about the topic of discussion. It is a wise management principle to get this individual involved by asking questions, such as, "You've been listening intently to everything that's been said without making any comments. What do you think?" Such comments will usually reveal some interesting thoughts that would have remained unspoken if you hadn't possessed the wisdom and knowledge to offer encouragement.

REASSURANCE

We are our own worst critics. As such, we sometimes need reassurance. Since we can't walk around with a security blanket like Linus from "Peanuts," we tend to develop reassurance gestures, of which we are usually unaware. The gestures adults use to reassure themselves are generally different from those of children and teens. For example, a young child may suck on his thumb, on a piece of fabric, or on a loose-fitting garment he is wearing. A teenager may bite his nails or pick up the habit of smoking.

A common adult reassurance gesture is rubbing one's thumbs together while the fingers of both hands are interlocked. A variation of this is cuticle picking or pinching the topside of the hand. Other reassurance gestures include placing a pen or pencil in one's mouth and perhaps biting it. (A paperclip or a piece of paper can serve the same purpose.) It has been observed that a person who is attending a meeting and needs reassurance that she belongs there will touch the back of the chair before sitting.

Another reassurance gesture is bringing a hand to one's throat or fingering a necklace. Quite often, someone will perform this gesture upon hearing something that makes her uncomfortable.

COOPERATION

The Roman emperor Marcus Aurelius once said, "We are born for cooperation, as are the feet, the hands, the eyelids, and the upper and lower jaws." And, indeed, that is true. If the parts of the human body didn't cooperate with one another, we would all be in dire straits. Likewise, to achieve certain goals, we need cooperation. If you are attempting to marshal assistance or form a cooperative group, it is extremely important to be aware of cooperative gestures.

Undoubtedly, there have been times when you sensed that someone was cooperating fully, only to have his manner suddenly change. It is very noticeable when a person's previously casual attitude toward you quickly becomes formal, and the friendly, relaxed smile becomes a frown. He is no longer interested in being cooperative. That's why it's so important to be aware of the other members of a team, and to act in a manner that keeps them involved and supportive.

Coauthors Hank and Jerry were once part of a negotiating team discussing a product of great scientific value. The issues involved were patent rights, equity position, royalties, research and development costs, and incentives for both their client and the company that was to manufacture and market the product. As soon as the discussion started, a member of the other side took a sprinter's position by sitting forward in his chair, with only the toes of his shoes touching the ground—just like a runner awaiting the start of a footrace. (See Figure 4.19.) Reading his body language was extremely important because he was the technical member of the other team, and his positive views and opinions would be necessary. His initial gestures told Hank and Jerry that he was very interested in what they had to present, and when he asked technical questions, they were adequately answered by the scientific members of their team.

Figure 4.19.
The Sprinter's Position.

In the initial seating arrangement, Hank and Jerry had chosen chairs that were close to this key participant in order to read him well. He became very cooperative once they had helped him overcome his initial doubts and had adequately answered his technical questions. Recognizing and capitalizing on his cooperative mannerisms and gestures brought about a successful conclusion that benefited both parties. Afterward, he went out of his way to compliment them on how well they had addressed all of his questions and reservations.

FRUSTRATION

Gestures that communicate frustration are generally the easiest to observe. If you have any doubt, simply watch a Sunday football game, and you will see a great amount of frustration displayed on the screen. On a play, the quarterback fades back and throws a forward pass that slips through his teammates "butter fingers." Upon missing the ball, the player kicks the ground in disgust and slaps the side of his helmet. If you are watching a baseball game and the batter strikes out by swinging at a bad pitch, he'll angrily toss the bat away and rub the back of his neck as he walks slowly to the dugout with his head bowed.

While non-baseball players may not throw bats to display their frustration, they do similarly rub the back of their necks and bow their heads. (See Figure 4.20.) Banging the table, breaking a pencil, stamping the foot, and other such behaviors are akin to kicking the dirt and throwing the bat. Another common sign of frustration is the "hot-under-the-collar" gesture (see Figure 4.21), which occurs when someone runs his fingers around the collar of a shirt.

Figure 4.20.

Rubbing the Neck in Frustration.

Sometimes, frustration isn't displayed through gestures. Instead, someone may exhibit this emotion through sounds, such as a heavy sigh or audible breath. A colleague of Hank and Jerry's had to work very hard to control his temper. Whenever he was close to reaching his "boiling point," he would begin to breathe rather heavily. This was a sign for them to cool things off or run the risk of having him lose his temper. A Texas rancher once told us that the first sound from an angry bull before it charges you is a snort. This is a warning that should be taken very seriously. Likewise, psychologists generally agree that people have a tendency to take short, heavy breaths through the nostrils when they are frustrated or angry. Like the snort from a bull, this is a warning. Another unmistakable sound to listen for is the "tsk" sound.

Figure 4.21.

Running Fingers Around the Collar in Frustration.

The "tsk" may also reflect astonishment, disgust, or regret, so use all the cues available to determine what it means. (A word of caution: In Syria, the "tsk" sound means "no" and is used regularly in conversation.)

When a person kicks an imaginary object on the ground, he is displaying yet another gesture of frustration. Do not confuse this with an individual who is concentrating on something very important while walking slowly. Occasionally, he may stop for a few moments to "kick things around" while contemplating matters and possible decisions.

It's possible for people to misinterpret frustration body cues, just as it's possible to misread other gestures. Because of this, it is wise to get verbal feedback to confirm an analysis of another's state of mind.

DISGUST

The most common disgust gesture is best described as turning up one's nose at something. This gesture clearly indicates dislike and rejection. Infants instinctively "turn up their nose" at food they dislike and pull back their heads as if to avoid an unpleasant odor. Adults move the head slightly backward and "look down their nose" at someone.

Turning away from someone—in other words, giving him the cold shoulder—also indicates disgust with what has been said or done. In the deaf community, since visual experience is essential for communication, turning one's back on someone who wishes to converse is the ultimate cold shoulder.

CONFIDENCE AND SELF-CONTROL

A confident person is likely to speak without using hand-to-mouth or hand-to-head gestures. Whenever you watch a self-assured person talk, you'll notice that he primarily uses his hands to emphasize what he is saying, and does not touch his face or head. You'll also notice that when standing, he takes a proud and erect stance, and never slouches. Moreover, you will seldom see a confident person shifting his body from side to side. This individual will also use a fair amount of eye contact.

A common hand gesture displayed by someone who is feeling self-assured is the steeple, discussed in Chapter 3 (see page 36). The steeple is performed by touching the fingertips of opposite hands together, creating a shape similar to that of a church tower. (See Figure 4.22.) People may use it when speaking or listening, and the hands may be held high or low. The low steeple, a more discreet variation of this gesture, is most commonly used by women. (See Figure 4.23.) The subtle steeple, another indication of confidence, looks similar to both the high and low steeples except that the hands are joined more closely, with one hand enclosing the fist of the other. (See Figure 4.24.) This confidence gesture is most often seen in business. However, the gesture is also used by those in the clergy, lawyers, doctors, and especially academicians, who seem to be very comfortable in this position while lecturing on a favorite subject.

Figure 4.22.
Using the Steeple.

Figure 4.23.
Using the Low Steeple.

Some people who unconsciously use the gesture place their steeple so high that they actually look at you through their fingers. This often makes others uncomfortable. Thus, continuing a conversation with a person who is doing this requires self-control. It may help you to recognize that most people are unaware of what they're doing. In some cases, if the steepling gesture is used by someone in a weak negotiating position, she gives the side with greater leverage the impression that there is more to her position than there truly is. Therefore, we rec-

Figure 4.24.
Using the Subtle Steeple.

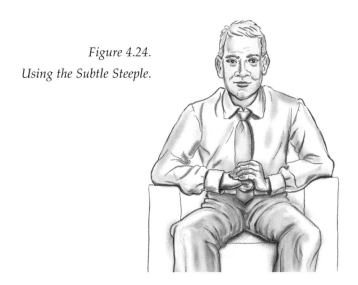

ommend that the next time your point is not as strong as you would like it to be, you steeple your fingertips, smile slightly, and say nothing. Then wait to see how the other party responds.

Another common confidence gesture is an erect stance with the hands clasped behind the back. (See Figure 4.25.) This gesture displays not only confidence but also authority, and is used by law-enforcement officers worldwide. If you were ever in the military, this gesture no doubt brings back memories of your drill sergeant. It is the picture of absolute power and pride.

Figure 4.25. A Stance of Authority.

DOMINANCE AND SUPERIORITY

There are numerous nonverbal gestures and postures that clearly define and illustrate superior and subordinate positions in every walk of life. For obvious reasons, these are especially prevalent and noticeable in the military. In many instances, the more aggressively a superior behaves, the more threatened and insecure the subordinate may feel and subsequently react.

Perhaps anthropologists would say that it's natural for men to be more territorial than women. However, both men and women are capable of nonverbally communicating their territorial rights. One such gesture that silently displays one's "superiority" over the group in a business dealing is a leg or foot up on the table. (See Figure 4.26.)

Territorial rights can also be conveyed by placing and/or spreading objects—such as books, papers, laptops, or purses—in a space, thereby prohibiting others from using that area. If you recall studying in a library as a student, you can clearly visualize how your peers would spread their notebooks and other possessions around the table and put something on a chair to discourage anyone from sitting near them. This plainly says, "I want privacy!" The late British psychiatrist Humphrey Osmond termed this *sociofugal space*. Most people attempt to create sociofugal space every day without knowing it. For example, sociofugal space is produced by draping a coat or sweater over the back of a seat to prevent others from sitting in it, or by getting into an elevator and immediately going to an empty corner, like a prizefighter entering a ring. In some cases, sociofugal space may be created to keep unwanted people from entering it so that it is open for a more desirable person. For example, a man may sit in an aisle seat on a train and place his briefcase on the window seat until he sees a pretty woman approaching, at which point he removes the briefcase and opens the way for her.

Figure 4.26.
The Foot-on-Table Gesture.

There is also an accepted sociofugal space—a comfortable distance—when standing face to face with someone. This distance differs by culture, and even according to the relationship of the two people involved. For instance, you can comfortably stand much closer to a husband or wife than you can to a mere acquaintance. If someone "gets in our space," we become uncomfortable. Always be aware of and maintain this polite distance to avoid making other people feel uneasy. (To learn more, see "The Sociofugal Space Invader" inset on page 84.)

Straddling a chair is another gesture that communicates authority and dominance. (See Figure 4.27.) A salesperson would not sit in such a position when making a sales call to a prospective buyer unless he wanted to blow the sale.

By towering over someone who is seated, you nonverbally communicate that you feel superior. (Perhaps that's how the expression "he feels head and shoulders above you" originated.) Elevating your body above others is an expression of dominance. For that very reason, the thrones of kings and queens are elevated. Many common expressions connote this elevated position—for example, "your highness," "on a pedestal," "look up to them," and "above the crowd." If an indi-

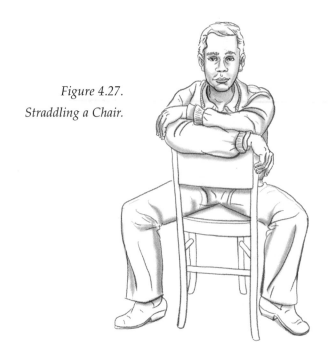

Figure 4.27.
Straddling a Chair.

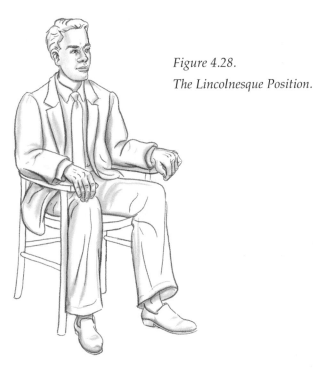

Figure 4.28.

The Lincolnesque Position.

vidual wishes to communicate dominance or superiority over some-one else, she will raise herself above the other person by standing over him while he is seated, or rise up from a seated position to tower over him. Be careful if you use this gesture. It usually elicits resentment in the other individual. If you want cooperation, it is better to meet some-one on even ground.

Nonverbal communication of equality and neutrality can best be illustrated by the Lincolnesque position, in which a person is seated with legs uncrossed, arms resting on the armrests, and coat unbut-toned. (See Figure 4.28.) This is an open and agreeable position. When two people are sitting across from each other in the Lincolnesque pos-ture, neither one is sending a nonverbal message of dominance.

SELF-SATISFACTION AND CELEBRATION

When someone is feeling satisfied, it is often shown in the way he leans back, hands clasped behind his head and legs crossed in the figure-four position. (See Figure 4.29.) This gives the impression that this person knows he is the one in control. In contrast, an indication that someone is feeling dejected is shown in the way he leans forward, shoulders slumped and arms limply supported at the knees. (See Figure 4.30.)

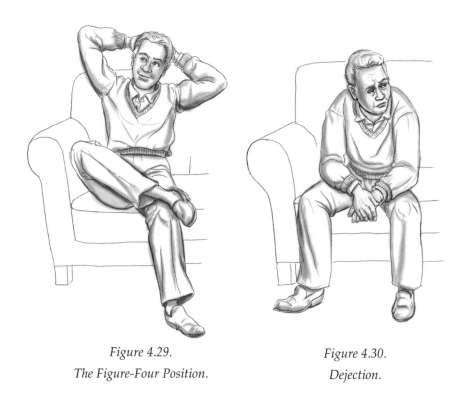

Figure 4.29.

The Figure-Four Position.

Figure 4.30.

Dejection.

A common sound made by a person who is feeling content, comfortable, and confident is the clucking sound, created when the tongue is raised to the roof of the mouth and released to drop quickly. You've probably heard the phrase, "She was so proud she clucked like a mother hen." This is a sound of self-satisfaction. Sometimes, the cluck is accompanied by a gesture, such as snapping the fingers of one hand and then, with an open palm of the same hand, tapping the closed fist of the other one as is if putting a cap on a bottle.

A common sign of satisfaction and celebration that may be seen when concluding a deal, for instance, is raising a fist in the air and vigorously moving it down a few inches, as if pulling the cord of an old-fashioned train whistle. This is sometimes to referred to as a fist pump. Another familiar gesture of celebration is the thumbs-up sign, in which a closed fist is held with the thumb extended upwards.

NERVOUSNESS

Some of the clearest signs of nervousness are not gestures or postures, as you would probably expect. Instead, a very reliable and discernible indicator is sound. When a person clears his throat just before speaking, or clears his throat mid-sentence, he is demonstrating anxiety and tension. Virtually anyone who has had to speak before a large group can recall a tight sensation in the throat before uttering the first words; this happens when mucus forms due to anxiety or apprehension. Therefore, it is natural to clear the throat before speaking. In some cases, people who are not accustomed to public speaking clear their throats continuously during their presentation. These individuals may also display changes in voice inflection and tone that reveal their uncertainty and doubt. Verbal tics—"like," "ah," "you know," and others—may also be apparent. The next time you clear your throat before speaking, take note of whether you are doing it out of nervousness or if you do, in actuality, need to clear your throat.

A sure-fire nonverbal sign of nervousness is fidgeting or squirming in a chair. During cross-examination, a good trial attorney will notice which questions get the witness "squirming." These are the questions he will return to for clarification. (See page 101 for more information on courtroom body language.)

A person who slowly rubs her hand against fabric, such as clothing or a handkerchief, is nonverbally illustrating anxiety, frustration, anger, nervousness, or uncertainty over a stressful situation. At such times, the palms of the hands usually become sweaty. One can often see such gestures when people are involved in a stressful activity such as testifying in court as a witness; making a speech for the first time; or, in the case of athletes, anxiously awaiting the start of a game or the beginning of a race. Such "sweaty palm" gestures may be observed daily, regardless of the temperature.

INSINCERITY AND ASTONISHMENT

Covering the mouth while speaking can be a gesture of astonishment, doubt, nervousness, deception, or a lack of confidence. (See Figure 4.31.) In other cases, a person may cover her mouth after saying something she wishes she hadn't said, almost as if she were attempting to shut off the flow of words that have already been spoken. Law-enforcement officials look at this gesture as an attempt to cover up the truth or fabricate a lie. Parents are very familiar with this gesture. When a child is trying to explain something and her hand goes up to her mouth, a parent instinctively knows that what's being said isn't truthful. When a child feels self-assured and confident about what she is saying, her hands are not near her mouth.

Figure 4.31.
Covering the Mouth
in Surprise.

Figure 4.32.
Covering the Mouth
in Secrecy.

"You Dirty Rat"

In the golden age of Hollywood, a male actor who wished to portray some-one who was underhanded wouldn't cover his mouth to imply secrecy when he spoke. Instead, he would talk out of the side of his mouth in a hushed tone. This gesture was always associated with convicts or ex-cons. Interest-ingly, this stereotype probably originated because prisoners who were not permitted to speak to each other circumvented the rule by talking out of the side of their mouths, which presumably became such an ingrained habit that it continued after they were released.

People who consciously wish to hide their conversations from pry-ing eyes will often cup a hand to the mouth. This is a gesture with which we are all familiar. Similarly, when someone who is seated places his elbows on the table with folded hands, essentially covering his mouth, his body language is saying, "I don't want you to hear me." He is trying to block his words and meaning. (See Figure 4.32.) This person will usually maintain this position while speaking or listening. When he is ready to be forthcoming, he will drop his hands.

Covering the mouth shouldn't be confused with gestures of inter-ruption, which indicate that someone wishes to interject a comment during a conversation. (For more information, see the inset "May I Interrupt?" on page 76.)

SELF-CONTROL

When we were children, many of us were told by parents and teach-ers to get a hold of ourselves—to exercise self-control and use it to overcome frustration, anxiety, or, most important, anger. As we grew up, we learned to discipline ourselves and keep our emotions at bay in a nondestructive manner. However, the nonverbal gestures we accu-mulated along the way can be very telling.

When someone is practicing self-control while standing or walking, he is likely to clasp both hands behind his back, with one hand clenched tightly while the other grips his wrist or arm. (See Figure 4.34. on page 78.) His body is clearly saying to the world that he is trying to control

"May I Interrupt?"

Virtually all of us wish to be great conversationalists. To be so, we need to be aware of the interrupt gesture so we can stop talking when we see it, and allow the listener to speak. During a conversation, we have the ability to listen to about 650 to 700 words per minute. However, even the most rapid speaker can say only about 150 to 160 words per minute. That leaves the listener with 75 percent of his listening time to evaluate, accept, or reject what's being said.

As children, we learned to raise our hand if we wished to speak. This idea has been ingrained in us. Although as adults we no longer have to raise our hand, the hand will often go up, not over our heads, but high enough to show that we have something to say or ask. Once a hand is raised four to six inches, it does not return to its original position. Instead, it goes to the head.

When a listener's hand rises, it primarily moves to two different locations on the face—to the earlobe or to the lips. When it goes to the earlobe (see Figure 4.33), you'll notice that the hand tugs slightly at the ear and then returns to its original position. However, when the hand goes to the mouth, you'll observe that the index finger is often lightly placed over the lips as if it were attempting to stop any words from pouring out. Sometimes, when the index finger remains in that position, the individual taps his index finger on his lips as he listens.

An individual occasionally restrains his interrupt gestures. Instead of touching part of his head, he may simply raise his hand a few inches, flick the fingers upward, and allow the hand to fall back to its original position, on either a thigh or a tabletop. Such interrupt gestures may be repeated several times without the person saying a single word. Unfortunately, interrupt gestures are often overlooked or ignored.

The talker and the listener each have a difficult task. If the speaker has been so motivational that the listener wants to be involved, it means that they have to change roles. In some situations, the speaker does not want to change roles. However, that is precisely what an expert conversationalist will do. He will carefully note the listener's gestures and facial expressions and will stop talking when the other person indicates that he wishes to say something.

Figure 4.33.
Tugging the Ear.

When a person places either hand on the speaker's forearm, bicep, or shoulder, he is using a more aggressive gesture to immediately interrupt the speaker. To soften this aggressive gesture, the person who is interrupting might say, "I'm sorry for interrupting you, but . . ." or "I agree with some of what you've said, but . . ."

Being aware of interrupt gestures and acknowledging them as signals of a listener's wish for involvement doesn't adversely affect your message. On the contrary, unless the interruption is destructive, the listener's input often tells you how well you're getting through to him, or lets you know about the specific areas of resistance that you need to be aware of before proceeding further in the conversation.

Whenever you positively react to a listener's interrupt gestures, he immediately considers you a great conversationalist because you have allowed him to participate in the communication process. The philosopher Zeno observed: "We have two ears and one mouth that we may listen more and talk the less."

Figure 4.34.
Practicing Self-Control
While Standing.

himself. When someone is practicing self-control while sitting, he will often lock his ankles, and may also clench his hands on the armrests of the chair. (See Figures 4.35 and 4.36, and note that men and women cross their ankles differently.) Airline attendants are adept at reading people. They can often tell which passengers are particularly apprehensive about flying because the passenger's ankles will usually be crossed—especially just before takeoff. Likewise, patients at the dentist's office are often observed locking their ankles when they sit down

Self-Control Out the Window?

A very angry, frustrated person who is unable to openly express his feelings may be observed scratching his head and/or rubbing his neck in an attempt to maintain self-control. He may also clench his fists or grab his own arm or wrist. If he's on his feet, he may even go so far as to narrow the distance between himself and the antagonist, hence the expression "eyeball-to-eyeball." If he's close to getting physical and still wishes to practice self-control, he may redirect his anger towards a substitute target by banging a table with his fist, slamming a door, or kicking an object.

for treatment. Perhaps in both cases, these people are controlling the desire to flee and avoid the unpleasantness! People often unconsciously display this crossed-ankle gesture during professional confrontations, as well. When matters settle down and things are moving in a more positive direction, they unconsciously uncross their legs.

Figure 4.35.

A Man Practicing Self-Control While Seated.

Figure 4.36.

A Woman Practicing Self-Control While Seated.

BOREDOM OR LACK OF INTEREST

At one time or another, we all become bored or uninterested in what's going on around us. How can we tell when others are bored? An almost sure-fire sign is a slight kicking motion of one foot while the legs are crossed. (See Figure 4.37.) This gesture is often seen when a person is waiting for something to happen, such as a plane departure or the end of a meeting.

Figure 4.37.

Kicking the Foot in Boredom.

Another sign of boredom or a lack of interest is the monotonous rhythmic drumming of fingers on a tabletop, or the repeated clicking of a pen. In some cases, these behaviors are unconscious, but in other cases, they are not. Whether conscious or unconscious, such sounds can be nerve-wracking to everyone in the vicinity of the bored individuals.

There are some mental health professionals who believe that when we are bored, impatient, or anxious, we attempt to duplicate a life experience that made us feel safe and secure—specifically, our time in the womb, when we heard our mother's comforting heartbeat. Whether or not it is true that repetitive motions recreate the rhythms of the heart, it is clear that during times of boredom or stress, many people nonverbally communicate their emotions by making repetitive sounds.

One associate of ours remembers a labor negotiator whom he called "the thumper" due to his habit of constantly banging his fingers on any hard surface he could find. He further told us that the negotiator's thoughts could be easily discerned by the speeding up or slowing down of his tempo. Whenever he was bored with the proceedings, he would thump at a fast rate, using all four fingers. However, when he was thoughtfully considering an offer or proposal, he used only the middle finger at a much slower thumping rate. When the negotiator was very close to concluding all of his objections, or perhaps ready to agree to a settlement, the thumping stopped completely, and the man would look at the ceiling for a while, take a very deep breath, and express something positive. Our friend told us he met the gentleman years later, when both were retired, and told him how he had "read him like a book." They both had a good laugh.

Perhaps the most obvious sign that someone is bored—whether he is listening to someone talk or watching a presentation—occurs when he rests his head on his hand and his eyelids become droopy. (See Figure 4.38.) Such a person is making no effort whatsoever to disguise his lack of interest in what is going on. On the other hand, a sign of boredom that is often misread is the "blank look." This look has been accurately described as the "I'm looking at you but not hearing a word you're saying" stare. It is a zombie-like gaze coming from a person you already suspected wasn't listening to you, and is now nearly asleep with his eyes open. As you may recall from Chapter 2, infrequently blinking eyes may indicate several things, including that the person isn't mentally present. There will usually also be a lack of eye movement when someone isn't paying attention.

When people in an audience fidget or squirm, it is assumed that they are bored. While this is potentially true, there are actually several possible reasons for fidgeting: 1) they are physically tired, 2) it is nearing lunchtime or they need to use the restroom or take a break, 3)

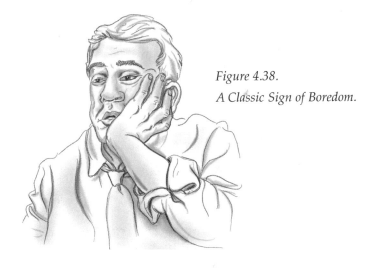

Figure 4.38.
A Classic Sign of Boredom.

they are uncomfortable, or 4) they are preoccupied with something of importance and are unable to concentrate. In fact, there are many potential reasons, so it is important to take into account other cues, nonverbal as well as verbal.

If you are addressing a group, it is essential to be aware of how your message is being accepted. Perhaps you've heard the question, "Why are you still talking when your audience has left?" In other words, don't be blind as to how your audience is receiving your speech. (For more information on talking to a group, see page 103 of Chapter 5.)

ACCEPTANCE

A common sign of acceptance is the hand-to-chest gesture that reveals a person's agreement with what someone else is saying, doing, or planning. (See Figure 4.39.) For centuries, people have been using this gesture to communicate loyalty, honesty, and devotion. In fact, this is what we do when we pledge allegiance to the flag of the United States. In a similar movement that goes back to ancient Rome, a salute of loyalty and acceptance is performed by holding one hand to the chest while the other is thrust outward toward the person being greeted.

Figure 4.39.
The Hands-to-Chest
Gesture of Acceptance.

Touching gestures that indicate acceptance are often used between people who are well known, liked, and loved (see Figure 4.40), and are seldom used between strangers or casual acquaintances. People who employ touch to communicate nonverbally usually have no difficulty revealing their emotions. The most commonly touched areas are the shoulders and arms. Touching can also be a calming gesture, usually accompanied by a spoken phrase such as, "Don't worry" or "Calm down."

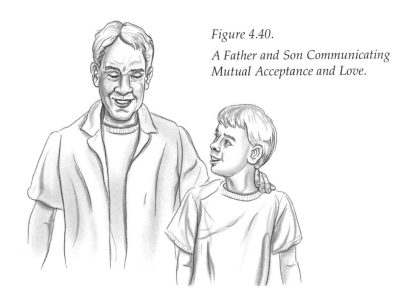

Figure 4.40.

A Father and Son Communicating Mutual Acceptance and Love.

When one person moves closer to another, narrowing the gap between them, he is likely communicating acceptance because he feels kinship, has something that he wants to share in confidence, or both. In some cases, of course, this closeness may actually make the other person feel uncomfortable. (See "The Sociofugal Space Invader" inset on page 84.)

Interestingly, the space between two deaf people who are communicating is usually wider than it would be between two non-deaf people. This is because deaf people need adequate space to clearly observe the simultaneous movements of the other person's face, hands, and body. Only when someone is finger-spelling an individual word is the focus solely on the hands. Normally, the focus is on the face, principally the mouth, with hand and body movements observed peripherally.

The Sociofugal Space Invader

As explained earlier in this chapter (see page 70), sociofugal space is the imaginary personal space surrounding an individual. As long as you remain outside a person's area of comfort, he will feel at ease. If you invade his space, however, he will immediately feel somewhat unnerved.

Most people do respect the sociofugal space of others. But some people, such as the so-called "close talker" (see Figure 4.41), have a tendency to violate that space and fail to notice the other person's reaction, which is usually to move back. Instead of reading this obvious gesture as "I'm uncomfortable with you that close" or "Stay out of my space," the close talker again narrows the distance. Even another step away may not get him to discontinue his "space pursuit." The best course of action in this case is to either end the conversation or be honest about the need for some breathing room. Always try to be acutely aware of how another person is reacting to your attempts at reducing the distance, and respond as necessary to maintain or restore a level of comfort.

Figure 4.41. The Close Talker.

EXPECTANCY

At one time or another, every one of us has nonverbally expressed our anticipation of receiving something. Regardless of an individual's age, unless the hands are cold due to the weather or clammy due to nervousness, the motion of rubbing one's palms together (see Figure 4.42) is a clear gesture of expectation. (Perhaps this is why so many crap-shooters consciously use the gesture when they are getting ready to throw dice in a game.) A child may rub his hands together upon seeing his mom pull up in a station wagon full of "goodies," and a sixty-year-old executive may use the same gesture upon learning that his company just landed a big account.

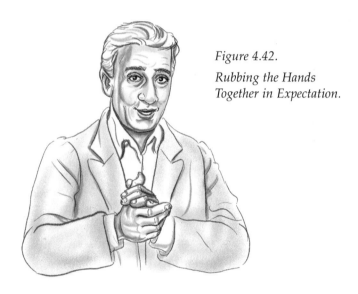

Figure 4.42.

Rubbing the Hands Together in Expectation.

Another gesture of expectancy is rubbing the thumb and index finger together in anticipation of receiving something such as money or a gift. Finally, employees in the service industry use a variety of gestures to express their desire for a tip. (See the inset "To Ensure Prompt Service" on page 86.)

ROMANTIC/SEXUAL INTEREST

Virtually all species have certain courtship rituals, and humans are no exception. Quite often, when a person is attracted to someone she encounters, she will unknowingly send out courtship signals. Prolonged eye contact, pupil dilation, broad smiles, preening motions such as smoothing the hair or clothing, tilting the head, closing the distance, crossing and uncrossing the legs, absently caressing one's own arm or leg, and light touching make up a complete array of "I'm attracted to you" gestures. This sets the stage for one of the parties to make the next move by verbally expressing interest.

To Ensure Prompt Service

Doormen, bellhops, restaurant servers, and other service personnel use a variety of expectation gestures to signal a desire to be tipped. These gestures range from the obvious jingling of coins to the "Ancient Egyptian" posture, in which the palm of the hand is turned upward behind the body. In other cases, the service person hesitates long enough to allow the idea of tipping to pop into the individual's head. One means of prolonging contact with the customer, and perhaps introducing the idea of a tip, is to use an expression such as, "I hope you have a great day!" or "Let's see if we can find a good table for your party tonight, sir!" Often when a person overlooks such expressions of expectation, the service is less than prompt.

CONCLUSION

As you can see, there is a lot to be aware of when you are trying to determine an attitude. It can be difficult to observe every individual gesture that makes up a complete cluster. However, observing even a few gestures can give you a good idea of someone's thoughts and intentions. It's like hearing only the most important words spoken in a long statement, and being capable of grasping the overall theme and meaning. In the next chapter, we will look at specific relationships and the importance of understanding body language.

5

Relationships
and Body Language

*"Circumstances are beyond the control of man;
but his conduct is in his power."*

—Benjamin Disraeli, *Contarini Fleming*

W hether you are in the presence of family members, romantic partners, business associates, or strangers, having a clear grasp of body language can help you better understand the situation and more effectively communicate your emotions and ideas. In this chapter, we'll discuss nonverbal gesture clusters as they relate to specific relationships. As you read the following descriptions and suggestions, try to recall specific interactions you've had with your own child, spouse, business associate, and others. Think about the function body language plays in your relationships, and then consider ways in which you might better use this mode of communication to enhance your dealings with everyone in your life.

PARENTS AND CHILDREN

During the first two years of life, sound is a child's principal means of communication with his parents. When he's hungry, wet, or otherwise uncomfortable, he cries or screams until his parents respond. But as a child grows and becomes socialized by those around him, he develops a repertoire of body language gestures that can convey a range of emotions. It's important for parents to be attuned to a child's gestures, expressions, and postures, as they are sometimes the only clues that the youngster is experiencing a problem.

Below, we'll consider body language that your child may use to communicate common emotions such as anger, fear, and happiness. Keep in mind that while some of these gestures may be found in children of nearly any age, some are more likely to occur in younger or older children. Generally, younger children more freely express emotions through obvious signals such as tantrums, while as children mature, they tend to use more subtle gestures. It is also important to use your understanding of your child and your knowledge of his activities to help you interpret his gestures. For instance, the slamming of a door may indicate excitement to get outside and play with a friend or, conversely, it may indicate anger and frustration.

Signs of Anger

- Stiffening of body.
- Tears and tantrums.
- Facial grimaces or sour expressions.
- Turning away from you.
- Angry slamming of doors or other objects.

Signs of Fear and Insecurity

- Thumb sucking.
- Clinging to you.
- Tense crossing of arms.
- Rigidity of shoulders and rest of body.
- Frozen (unchanging) facial expression.

Signs of Happiness and Self-Confidence

- Smiling and laughing.
- Relaxed body position.
- Standing very close to you when conversing.
- Animated, exuberant body movements.

As your child grows, you will want to see a balance of different emotions. It's normal for your child to sometimes be fearful or angry, but this should be balanced with times of joy and happiness. If negative body language seems to outweigh positive gestures, don't ignore the signs, but try to find the root cause so that your child can learn to constructively handle fear and anger, and enjoy more periods of happiness and calm.

MARRIED COUPLES

For some reason, most people have difficulty reading those who are the closest to them, even when they are generally on the same wavelength. People tend to take their most intimate relationships for granted, and as a result, nonverbal communication may suffer. We strongly recommend that no matter how well you think you know someone, whether a spouse or other romantic partner, you make every effort to listen to what he is saying and note his body language, which is often more revealing than words. Many marriage counselors assert that most marital problems begin with a breakdown in communication. Correctly hearing and observing the other person is vital in maintaining a good marriage.

In Japan, prior to the second half of the twentieth century, a wife would not verbalize her displeasure with her husband. Instead she would nonverbally communicate her feelings through her flower arrangements. When the husband arrived home after work, he was to look at the flower arrangement to determine his wife's mood and how to approach her. Considering the increasing number of separations and divorces that take place in the United States, there might be a lesson here.

On the next page, we list some of the gestures that your partner may use to communicate the common emotions of love and anger. When considering these signs, keep in mind that some people are more demonstrative than others, especially when other people are around. While one person may express affection by draping his arm around his wife, another may use more subtle gestures, such as leaning towards her as he speaks. People may also vary in their communication of displeasure and anger. Use your knowledge of your partner to help you interpret his gestures.

▇ Signs of Love and Affection

- Sitting or standing close to you.

- Leaning towards you while talking to you.

- Holding your hand.

- Placing his arm around your shoulders.

- Frequently touching your hand, arm, or shoulder.

- Frequently making eye contact.

▇ Signs of Anger or Resentment

- An icy silence.

- Stiffening of the body.

- Turning away from you.

- Maintaining a distance from you.

- Tightening or pursing of lips.

- Crossing of arms and/or legs.

- Placing of hands on hips.

- Angry slamming of doors or other objects.

Just as a child's gestures of anger should not be ignored, so should signs that your partner is annoyed or angry. By learning to read his body language, you will be able to re-establish communication and address issues in a timely and constructive manner.

PARTYGOERS AND PEOPLE AT OTHER SOCIAL GATHERINGS

In Chapter 1, you learned that an airport is a great place to hone your observation skills. Similarly, a party is a wonderful place to not only observe others, but also to use what you have learned about the meaning of body positions and gestures. Let's talk about some of the body language you may see at a social gathering.

It is not uncommon for married women to pair off with other married women, and married men to pair off with other married men at parties. People who are single tend to keep an eye out for other singles, even when they are already conversing with someone.

Couples who are dating seldom wander far from one another, often touching each other affectionately. Married couples with a very close bond can also be seen showing signs of affection. It's relatively easy to analyze which couples have been married for the shortest time. Couples who are still relatively new at marriage have a tendency to hold one another around the waist or walk hand in hand. This behavior silently communicates to everyone, "Hands off! She's (or he's) mine!" Touching someone is also a territorial sign.

Figure 5.1 shows two couples who are clearly enjoying each other's company. You'll notice that in one figure, the woman has placed her arm around her partner's neck in a show of affection, while in the other, the man has his arm around the woman's neck. As mentioned earlier, some people are more demonstrative of their feelings than others. Usually, one member of the couple is more comfortable than the other in physically expressing fondness when other people are in the room.

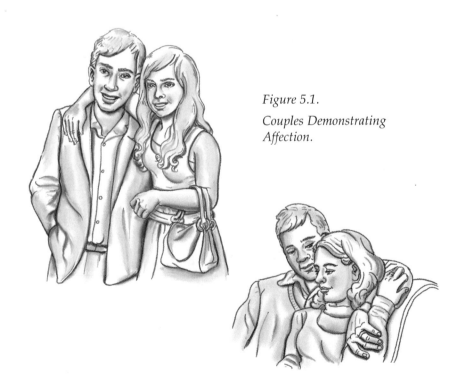

Figure 5.1.

Couples Demonstrating Affection.

When a couple has an argument prior to attending a function and fails to resolve the issue before the gathering, the partners tend to act extremely formal with each other, and any smiles they exchange are contrived ones, like the oblong smile. (See page 23.) Married or not, people who are upset with each other do not exchange touches very often, and when physical contact is made, the person being touched tends to recoil ever so slightly. Moreover, if the man and woman sit on the same couch during the gathering, they usually position themselves a little apart rather than cozying up to each other. (See Figure 5.2.)

Figure 5.2.
A Couple with an Unresolved Problem.

If you were in a roomful of people attending a social function, and noticed two individuals suddenly narrowing the distance between each other as they spoke, you would immediately think they were communicating something confidential. If you looked closer, you might also notice that instead of standing side by side, they had changed positions to face each other. These people are sending the nonverbal message, "This is personal, so don't interrupt!"

In many instances, watching people at a party or other social function can be as much fun as being a participant. It can be very entertaining to read the interpersonal, nonverbal communication that occurs. However, it is more important to be an active "player" who can read body language and react accordingly to make the most out of all social encounters. For instance, if you were alone at a party and saw another person in which you were interested, how would you determine if that person was open to getting to know you? Here are a few of the common gestures you might encounter:

■ Signs That Someone Is Not Open to Conversation

- Lack of eye contact.
- Maintaining physical distance from you.
- Leaning away from you.
- Tense stance or crossing of arms and/or legs.
- Distant or "closed" facial expression.

■ Signs That Someone Is Open to Conversation

- Making eye contact.
- Clearing of throat as if preparing to speak.
- Closing distance between you.
- Facing in your direction or leaning towards you.
- Relaxed stance, with no crossing of arms or legs.
- Open, smiling facial expression.

In the earlier sections on interpreting the body language of your children and significant other, we encouraged you to consider each individual's personality rather than just the isolated gestures. When viewing a stranger's posture and motions, it's important to recognize that your lack of familiarity with this person may lead you to incorrectly interpret her attitude. While her gestures may seem to indicate that she is not interested in you, for instance, she may simply be shy, so don't be afraid to take a chance and make contact. If you appear relaxed and open, and can casually deliver a nonthreatening, engaging comment, you may soon find yourself involved in a rewarding conversation.

SUPERVISORS AND EMPLOYEES

The average working relationship commonly involves a good deal of verbal communication, whether in the form of spoken or written words. But, as in every other association, supervisors and employees also "speak" through gestures, and it pays to be aware of these gestures and make them work for you.

It is, of course, vital for an employee to be able to read his boss's negative facial expressions, such as raised eyebrows, the slight twisting of the head, a look of doubt when he doesn't accept an idea, or failure to meet the employee's eyes. If these nonverbal messages aren't clue enough that the boss is displeased with the employee, he may resort to additional nonverbal clues, such as looking at his wristwatch (see Figure 5.3), sighing deeply, or shifting his weight. The ability to read and anticipate a manager's attitude is a wonderful asset.

No Time to Say Hello, Goodbye, I'm Late ...

Due to the vast number of people walking to and fro in large cities, most people keep to themselves. There's no time to exchange smiles, let alone stop and chat with strangers. In addition, there are cultural differences between various areas of the country. One woman who was flying from Atlanta to New York City remarked, "In Atlanta, everyone takes the time to look at others and smile occasionally." The same wasn't true of New York, she observed. While it's true that in less densely populated areas, nonverbal signals of friendship and hospitality on the street are more commonplace, it's important to recognize that the outward appearance and behavior of some city folk may simply be that—outward appearance. Over and over again, in times of crisis such as 9/11, the seemingly indifferent people of big cities have shown a sincere concern in those around them, including total strangers.

Figure 5.3.
An Unhappy Supervisor.

It is also essential for a manager to have the ability to interpret the nonverbal language of his employees and respond to it appropriately. A supervisor and his employees have a common goal and in order to be productive, a good relationship must be maintained. If an employee is angry, resentful, skeptical of a policy, or just plain bored, it will interfere not only with his work but also with the morale of the other members of the staff.

The following lists provide a quick guide to some of the gestures that you may see in the workplace:

Signs of a Manager's Anger or Skepticism

- Failure to make eye contact.
- Clenched hands.
- Raised eyebrows.
- Peering over the rim of eyeglasses (see page 51).
- Rubbing the back of the neck (see page 64).
- Running his fingers around the collar of his shirt (see page 65).
- Stern expression or look of doubt.
- Glancing at watch.
- Deep sighing.

◼ Signs of an Employee's Frustration or Defensiveness

- Failure to make eye contact.
- Clenched hands.
- Crossed arms of defensiveness, possibly with clenched fists (see page 35).
- Crossed legs of defensiveness (see page 46).
- Rubbing the face or eye in doubt (see page 56).
- Rubbing the back of the neck (see page 64).
- Running his fingers around the collar of his shirt (see page 65).

◼ Signs of an Employee's Boredom

- Kicking foot in impatience (see page 80), tapping pen on desk, or other repetitive motion.
- Resting head on hand, with half-open eyelids (see page 81).
- Daydreaming with a far-away facial expression.

◼ Signs of a Manager's or Employee's Satisfaction

- Making eye contact.
- Open, smiling facial expression.
- Relaxed stance, with no crossing of arms or legs.
- Leaning towards the other person during conversation.
- Hand-to-chest gesture of acceptance (see page 82).
- Lincolnesque posture (see page 71) showing relaxed attitude.

If you sense that your employer or employee is dissatisfied, bored, or angry, do not allow the situation to fester. Instead, act on your assessment of his body language and seek to resolve the problem before it can damage your relationship or productivity.

THE PROFESSIONAL-CLIENT RELATIONSHIP

The relationship between a professional and his client is one of the most sensitive of associations. Successful attorneys, accountants, consultants, and other professionals understand the importance of communication through body language. On the other hand, less-successful professionals seem unable to send the simple signals that build good rapport.

Any professional approaching a client for the first time should keep certain things in mind. When a client seeks professional help from someone new, it is possible that he is dubious about the individual's skills, but that he wants to be able to rely on the professional for solid advice. It is also probable that he will distrust simple advice because, like many clients, he may firmly believe that his situation is unique. To further complicate the relationship, he may be able to hear only what he wants to hear, and be unprepared to receive any negative comments from the professional. All of these factors can make the professional's role treacherous.

How can a professional avoid causing a client concern, and instead build a constructive relationship? One way in which the professional can create a feeling of security on the part of the customer is to take notes on what the client is saying. Whether or not the consultant feels that the client's words are important, this will make the customer feel that his unique situation is being recognized and noted. The professional can also make the client feel he's paying attention by using one of the gestures of evaluation discussed on pages 46 to 51. For instance, he can lean slightly forward with his head tilted to one side, perhaps supporting his head on one hand. This nonverbally communicates not only that the client's words are of great interest, but also that he is thinking of ways to help the customer.

As important as it is to use certain positive body language when working with a client, it is equally vital to avoid using negative gestures. When a consultant sits back in his chair, perhaps while using an aloof steepling gesture (see page 36), it may be interpreted as a sign of indifference by the client. If he happens to be seated behind a very large desk, it may be seen as another signal that he is not on the same side as the customer. That is why it is increasingly common for professionals and clients to meet on common ground, such as a conference table. The consultant also must communicate that he is an expert without seeming arrogant or implying that the customer is less intelligent than he is. Gestures such as holding the lapels of his jacket may convey a sense of self-importance, which can damage his relationship with the client.

The following lists provide a quick guide to some of the negative and positive gestures that may occur in the professional-client relationship.

Signs That a Client Is Doubtful or Worried

- Tense, closed body position, possibly with crossed legs or arms.
- Clenched hands.
- Critical evaluation gesture, with index finger extended along side of face (see page 48).
- Turning away from consultant, with sideways glance (see page 53).
- Touching the nose in doubt (see page 54).
- Rubbing the face in doubt (see page 55).
- Rubbing the eye in doubt (see page 56).

Signs That a Client Is Secure and Satisfied

- Relaxed, open body position, with no crossing of arms or legs.
- Lack of face touching.
- Evaluation gesture (see page 47).

Counterproductive Gestures of a Professional/Consultant

- Sitting back in chair with self-satisfied attitude.
- Steeple position of superiority (see page 36).
- Foot up on desk in gesture of arrogance (see page 69).
- Fingering lapels of jacket.

Productive Gestures of a Professional/Consultant

- Lincolnesque posture (see page 71) showing open, relaxed attitude.
- Taking notes.
- Making eye contact.
- Evaluation gesture (see page 47) or chin-stroking evaluation gesture (see page 49).

Note your client's body language from the first moments of your meeting. If you feel that he is communicating doubt or unease, reassure him using both words and your own positive body language. If you are successful, you will soon see gestures indicating that your client is more relaxed and receptive to your professional advice.

BUYERS AND SELLERS

As every successful salesperson knows, body language—both the ability to assess that of the buyer, and the skill to control your own—can mean the difference between making a sale and losing it. Buyers, too, know that a salesperson's gestures and movements can make them feel at ease, or completely turn them off to the proposed products and services.

In many sales transactions, both the buyer and seller adopt "win-lose" attitudes that elevate any negative emotions which already exist. As an example of this, a buyer may sit back in his chair, glare at the seller, and cross his arms and legs suspiciously, saying, "What are you selling?" This may prompt the seller to move forward in his chair and eagerly assume the sprinter's position, first discussed on page 62. But if the buyer dislikes a hard sell, he will probably withdraw and become defensive. If the seller then becomes insecure because his ideas are not being accepted, he may show classic defensive body language such as crossed arms, crossed legs, or even turning away from the buyer. Quickly, the situation can go from bad to worse.

A skilled salesperson quickly assesses the buyer and his body language. Is he sitting in a relaxed, informal posture in his chair? Is he assuming a more formal or closed posture? Once the salesperson determines the buyer's attitude, he can adapt his own approach. If the man is relaxed and appears to have a sense of humor, perhaps an initial joke would warm up the meeting. If the buyer is more serious and formal, the seller should probably stick to his traditional sales opening.

Of course, the salesman should also use his own body language to communicate a friendly, open manner. Some salespeople consciously mirror the position of the buyer—crossed arms and tilted head, for instance—as this puts many people at ease, paving the way for a successful sales pitch.

It is necessary for the salesperson to use gestures and body positions to "close the gap" between buyer and seller. Mirroring the other person's position and gestures can begin the job. Once the buyer warms up, the seller can further close the distance by providing materials for the buyer's perusal, perhaps even moving to the buyer's side of the table or desk as he describes his product. In this case, the seller must be aware of nonverbal signals indicating that the buyer doesn't appreciate such close proximity. If the buyer moves backwards in his chair, leans away, or worse, shifts his chair, it is time for the seller to restore the original space.

The lists below provide an at-a-glance guide to some of the negative and positive gestures that may occur in the buyer-seller relationship.

▨ Signs That a Buyer Is Defensive or Uninterested

- Tense, closed body position, with crossed legs or arms.

- Glaring or otherwise displeased or closed facial expression.

- Critical evaluation gesture, with index finger extended along side of face (see page 48).

- Turning away from consultant, with sideways glance (see page 53).

- Touching the nose in doubt (see page 54).

- Rubbing the face in doubt (see page 55).

- Rubbing the eye in doubt (see page 56).

▨ Signs That a Buyer Is Open and Interested

- Relaxed body position, with no crossing of arms or legs.

- Open, smiling facial expression.

- Lack of face touching.

- Making eye contact.

- Evaluation gesture (see page 47).

▨ Counterproductive Gestures of a Seller

- Tense, closed body position, with crossed legs or arms.

- Using the sprinter's position (see page 62) before the buyer is interested.

- Closing the space between the buyer and seller too quickly.

◼ Productive Gestures of a Seller

- Relaxed, open body position.
- Open, smiling facial expression.
- Mirroring (matching) the buyer's body language to increase feeling of ease.
- Once buyer is interested, moving closer and providing materials for buyer's perusal.

Like so many interactions, the buyer-and-seller relationship is a type of a dance. The seller takes the lead, but he must be sensitive to the responses of the buyer and choose his moves carefully so that the buyer is successfully "wooed" by the seller's approach.

PARTIES IN A COURTROOM

Everything that is said in a court of record is transcribed, and if an error has been committed by the judge or one of the lawyers, it can later be subject matter raised on appeal. But for many years, lawyers and judges have realized that there are numerous forms of nonverbal communication that may express true and unadulterated feelings. These observations do not become part of the record as words do, but can nevertheless have an effect on the course of the trial.

There are many successful attorneys who use their awareness of nonverbal communication to evaluate their colleagues, witnesses, and members of the jury. Former Judge James C. Adkins once stated that in jury selection, some lawyers consciously evaluate gestures that communicate an individual's characteristics and attitudes. Louis Katz wrote, "If a prospective juror keeps his fist clenched and spreads his hands out whenever the other attorney is talking, the first lawyer had better not keep the juror." Judge Katz further believes that hands nonverbally communicate whether a juror or potential juror is open-minded, hostile, or prosecution-minded. Jury members themselves, who are perhaps less conscious than trial attorneys, still rely on gestures to some degree whenever they appraise evidence in a case.

Clearly, it is essential that judges and trial lawyers become familiar with body language so that they can interpret the gestures of others and use their own gestures to best advantage. Below, we list some of the gestures—both negative and positive—that attorneys and jurors may display in the average courtroom.

▨ Signs That a Juror Is Open to the Attorney's Statements

• Open posture, with no crossing of arms or legs.

• Lincolnesque posture (see page 71) showing relaxed attitude.

• Tilted head and attentive expression, as in evaluation gesture (see page 47) or chin-stroking evaluation gesture (see page 49).

▨ Signs That a Juror Is Doubtful of or Hostile to an Attorney's Statements

• Closed posture, with arms and/or legs crossed.

• Distant or "closed" facial expression.

• Clenched hands.

• Rubbing the face or eyes in doubt (see pages 55 and 56).

• Critical evaluation gesture (see page 48).

• Wrinkled brow showing confusion.

▨ Counterproductive Gestures of an Attorney

• Lack of eye contact with jurors.

• Overreliance on notes, causing him to look down.

• Crossing arms, and thus cutting himself off from the jurors.

• Keeping hands in pockets as if he's hiding something.

• Remaining "frozen" in one body position or one spot in the courtroom.

▨ Productive Gestures of an Attorney

• Maintaining strong eye contact with jurors.

- Keeping arms uncrossed and out of pockets.

- Using hands to make natural gestures that emphasize what is being said.

- Closing the distance between attorney and jurors by moving closer to them.

- Mirroring (matching) the jurors' facial expressions and postures.

While it is important for attorneys to control their own body language and to observe that of the jurors, a caveat is in order. A juror's gestures and postures should never be viewed in isolation, separate from his responses to questions asked during jury selection. This is important because juror body language can be especially deceiving. Why? Most jurors view the process of selection as being boring—a hurry-up-and-wait process. Thus, any looks of boredom or exasperation may be their reaction to the courtroom procedure itself, and not to what the lawyer is saying. Also, jurors sometimes have their own agenda. They may, for instance, want to be liked and picked for the jury, and therefore make every effort to seem attentive and nonjudgmental. On the other hand, they may want to avoid serving on the jury, and therefore intentionally present a surly facial expression. Many attorneys find it more valuable to note the jurors' microexpressions. First discussed on page 26, microexpressions are involuntary expressions that flash on the face for only a brief instant. Experience has taught many attorneys that these "glimmers"—a momentary flush or grimace, for instance—may reveal more about the juror's attitude than his body position or deliberate facial expression.

SPEAKERS AND AUDIENCE MEMBERS

The prospect of speaking in front of a large group can be somewhat frightening because there is always the possibility that you will bore the audience. It's no wonder that some people get stage fright or "butterflies." This will probably inspire you to take the time to prepare a presentation of interest. But regardless of how good your preparation has been, during the actual speech, it is important to note the reaction of the audience and change your style as necessary to keep your listeners engaged in you and your topic.

As soon as you utter your first words, be aware of your audience's nonverbal feedback. If you detect any negative reaction, consider telling a humorous story or a joke that most of the audience members will understand and perhaps identify with. Humor makes a listener more receptive to what the speaker has to say.

One of the first audience gestures you should look for is one of critical evaluation, first discussed on page 48. People who display this gesture are waiting to be convinced that you have something worthwhile to say. The fewer of these gestures you see, the more success you are having. On the other hand, if you see the tilted head of evaluation (see page 47), you will know that the audience is actively listening to and interested in your presentation. If you detect gestures indicating that you are *not* having success getting your ideas across, or that the group has little interest in what you are saying, you can quickly change your format by, perhaps, asking questions of the group. Once the group is re-engaged, you can return to your unfinished presentation.

Be aware that there may be times when the material you are presenting to a group is very interesting, but the group has gone into "overload" because too much information has been presented at one time. As a result, your audience may temporarily be turned off because they are unable to absorb anything further. At this point, their gestures will clearly indicate a lack of interest to additional information. Their heads will become erect instead of tilted, and their backs will straighten up, rather than leaning forward. They will glance at their watches, at the ceiling, or at each other, and often position their bodies so that they are pointed in the direction of an exit. Whenever a group has reached this stage, remember the wisdom in the question: "Why are you still talking when your audience has left?" Take a cue from your audience and be prepared to change things up to re-engage their attention.

■ Signs That an Audience Is Bored or Skeptical

- Lack of eye contact.
- Tense crossing of arms and/or legs.
- Slightly repositioning the body away from you and toward another point, such as the exit.
- Distant or "closed" facial expression.

- Glancing around the room, at their watches, or at each other.

- Rubbing the face or eye in doubt (see pages 55 and 56).

- Kicking the foot in impatience (see page 80).

- Resting head on hand, with half-open eyelids, (see page 81).

- Gesture of critical evaluation (see page 48).

Signs That an Audience Is Interested and Engaged

- Maintaining eye contact.

- Sitting so that body is directly facing you.

- Relaxed body position, with no crossing of arms or legs.

- Tilted head and open, attentive expression, as in evaluation gesture (see page 47) or chin-stroking evaluation gesture (see page 49).

- Facial expression that changes according to topic being discussed, showing responsiveness.

Counterproductive Gestures of a Speaker

- Lack of eye contact with audience members.

- Overreliance on notes, causing her to look down all the time or to quickly glance up only to look down again.

- Remaining "frozen" in one body position or one spot on the stage.

- Lack of facial expression or unchanging expression.

- Keeping arms crossed, thrust into pockets, stiffly holding cards, or rigidly held at sides.

Productive Gestures of a Speaker

- Maintaining eye contact with the audience.

- Moving around the stage to address different portions of the audience. (Be aware that this will also help you relax.)

- Using varied, appropriate facial expressions.

- Using hands to make natural gestures that emphasize what is being said.

In reading the above clues and pointers, you probably gathered that it is vital to be able to rely on your memory—not your notes—as you speak. Cards are a great way to jog your memory if you suddenly draw a blank, but only by learning your speech in advance will you be able to make eye contact with audience members, move around the stage, use arm gestures, and otherwise close the distance between yourself and your listeners.

CONCLUSION

In this chapter, you've learned the importance of nonverbal communication in a variety of relationships. From intimate associations to business dealings, we all speak volumes to one another without necessarily uttering a word. You should now be more aware of the nonverbal messages that people are sending to you. Just as important, you should fully appreciate the impact that your own body language may be having on others. Take a moment to observe yourself in a mirror. Are you smiling, or frowning and strained? Do you look stern and disapproving, or pleasant and approachable? Now, think of your most common body postures. Do you sit in a way that expresses defensiveness or anger, or does your position convey a friendly, open attitude? By using your own nonverbal language effectively, you can improve all your relationships and bring out the best in family members, business associates, and even strangers.

Conclusion

ou've come a long way since you first opened this book, and now it's time to immerse yourself in a variety of real-life situations. Your everyday activities will be your laboratory, and your current relationships and those you will ultimately develop will be your experiments. You now have sufficient knowledge on hand to move forward with your studies. You'll discover that the more you use your abilities and hone your instincts, the better your abilities will become. All skills require development, and the reading of body language is no different.

It's a good idea to share your newly gained insights with those who are close to you, as well as with those who may oppose you. Keep in mind, too, that an understanding of body language can be used in a variety of ways. We hope you will use the information you have acquired to better respond to those around you, to present yourself in a more beneficial light, and to work with others to effectively solve problems.

You now know that there is much more to a person than what he says with words, and sometimes, even more than he shows through his facial expressions. This insight alone will make you more aware of everyone around you, which, in turn, will make others feel more appreciated and better understood. The result will be more effective, positive communication with everyone in your life.

Bibliography

Adler, Alfred. *Understanding Human Nature.* Oxford, England : Oneworld Publications, 2009.

Allport, Gordon W. *Studies in Expressive Movement.* Edinburgh, United Kingdom: Johnston Press, 2007.

Ambady, N., and Rosenthal, R. "Half a minute: Predicting teacher evaluations from thin slices of nonverbal behavior and physical attractiveness." *Journal of Personality and Social Psychology*, 64(3), 431-441, 1993.

Argyle, Michael. *The Psychology of Interpersonal Behaviour*, Fifth Edition. New York: Penguin, 1994.

Bacon, Albert M. *A Manual of Gesture.* Whitefish, MT: Kessinger Publishing, 2008.

Berne, Eric. *Games People Play.* New York: Ballantine Books, 1996.

Birdwhistell, Ray L. *Kinesics and Context.* Philadelphia: University of Pennsylvania Press, 1970.

Bruner, Jerome; Goodnow, Jacqueline; and Austin, George. *A Study of Thinking.* Edison, NJ: Transaction Publishers, 1986.

Cherry, Colin. *On Human Communication*, Revised Edition. Cambridge, MA: The MIT Press, 1980.

Darwin, Charles. *The Expression of the Emotions in Man and Animals.* New York: Penguin Classics, 2009.

Darwin, Charles. *On the Origin of Species.* New York: Dover Publications, 2009.

Fast, Julius. *Body Language,* Revised Edition. New York: M. Evans and Company, 2002.

Fromm, Erich. *The Forgotten Language.* New York: Henry Holt & Co., 1976.

Goffman, Erving. *Behavior in Public Places.* New York: The Free Press, 1966.

Goffman, Erving. *Interaction Ritual.* New York: Pantheon, 1982.

Grayson, Gabriel. *Talking With Your Hands, Listening With Your Eyes.* Garden City Park, NY: Square One Publishers, 2003.

Hall, Edward T. *The Hidden Dimension.* Gloucester, MA: Peter Smith Publisher, 1992.

Hayakawa, S.I., and Hayakawa, Alan R. *Language in Thought and Action.* Harvest, 1991.

James, William. *The Principles of Psychology.* New York: Cosimo Classics, 2007.

Jung, Carl Gustav. *Man and His Symbols.* New York: Dell, 1968.

Koch, Rudolf. *The Book of Signs.* New York: Dover Publications, 1955.

Korzybski, Alfred. *Manhood of Humanity.* Dodo Press, 2008.

Lorenz, Konrad. *King Solomon's Ring.* New York: Routledge, 2002.

Lorenz, Konrad. *On Aggression.* New York: Routledge, 2002.

Maslow, Abraham Harold. *Motivation and Personality.* New York: Harper Collins, 1987.

Morris, Desmond. *The Human Zoo.* New York: Kodansha Globe, 1996.

Morris, Desmond. *The Naked Ape.* Delta, 1999.

Nierenberg, Gerard, and Calero, Henry H. *The New Art of Negotiating.* Garden City Park, NY: Square One Publishers, 2009.

Ogden, C.K., and Richards, I.A. *The Meaning of Meaning.* Mariner Books, 1989.

Ortega Y Gasset, José. *Man and People.* New York: W.W. Norton and Company, 1963.

Sommer, Robert. *Personal Space,* Updated. Bristol, United Kingdom: Bosko Books, 2008.

Sullivan, Harry Stack. *The Psychiatric Interview.* W.W. Norton & Co, 1970.

Woolbert, C.H. "The Audience." *Psychological Monographs* 21, 1916.

About the Authors

Gerard I. Nierenberg, a successful lawyer, pioneered the idea of the "everybody wins" philosophy—now usually referred to as "win-win"—which ensures that all parties benefit from the negotiation process. Nierenberg has written twenty best-selling books, including *The New Art of Negotiating*, and is the founder of The Negotiation Institute, which offers state-of-the-art training to business and professional organizations, governments, and executives around the world.

Henry H. Calero has been writing about communication and negotiation for over thirty years. While taping negotiation workshops, Calero accumulated a wealth of information about gestures, postures, and expressions. After subsequent study, he became a leader in the field of body language. A consultant and writer for professional, academic, and technical publications, Calero is also author of *The Power of Nonverbal Communication* and coauthor of Nierenberg's *The New Art of Negotiating*.

Gabriel Grayson is the chairperson of the Sign Language Department at New School University in New York City, and is a principal court-appointed sign language interpreter for the NYC judicial system. As an expert in sign language and the son of deaf parents, Grayson has a unique understanding of body language. He is also the best-selling author of *Talking With Your Hands, Listening With Your Eyes*.

Index

crossed-legs position, 45, 46, 53
edge-of-chair position, 59
figure-four position, 71, 72
foot-on-table position, 69
kicking motion of foot, 79, 80
leg-on-the-table position, 69
leg-over-arm-of-chair position, 45, 46
Lincolnesque position, 71
readiness position, 58
sideways-turning position, 53
squirming, 73, 81–82
straddling position, 45, 70
Slumping of shoulders, 39
Smiles, 22–23
Social gatherings, 90–94
Sociofugal space, 69–70, 83, 84
Sounds
    as sign of frustration, 64–65
    as sign of nervousness, 73
    as sign of satisfaction, 72
Speaking
    covering mouth while, 73–75
    out of side of mouth, 75
    See also Conversation; Lying,
    signs of; Speechmakers and
    audience, body language
    between.
Speechmakers and audience, body
    language between, 103–105. *See
    also* Audience awareness when
    speaking.
Squinting, 18, 19, 48
Squirming, 73, 81–82
Standard handshake, 30
Standing postures as body language
    hands-clasped-behind-back
    position, 75, 78
    hands-on-hips position, 57–58
    showdown position, 60
    and sociofugal space, 70
    stance of authority, 68
    towering over others, 70–71
Staring, 16
Steepling of fingers, 36, 37, 66–68
Strutters, 41, 42
Study in Scarlet, A (Doyle), 1

Subtle steeple, 66, 67. *See also*
    Steepling of fingers.
Superior-inferior handshake, 32–33
Superiority and dominance, gestures
    indicating, 32–33, 68–71. *See also*
    Confidence and self-control,
    gestures indicating.
Supervisors and employees, body
    language between, 94–96
Surprise, gestures indicating, 73–75
Suspicion, gestures indicating, 52–57
Sweaty palms, 73

Talking. *See* Speaking.
Teeth, clenching of, 26. *See also*
    Mouth.
Telephone, postures when speaking
    on a, 4–6
Television-watching as means of
    honing observation skills, 10
Territorial rights, body language of,
    69
"Thinker, The" (Rodin), 48
Thumbs, rubbing together of, 62
Thumbs-up gesture, 33, 72
Touching head and face, 54–56,
    73–75, 76. *See also* Evaluation
    gestures.
Touching others, 38
Travelers, interpreting body
    language of, 4–7
"Tsk" sounds, 64–65
Tugging ear, 76, 77
Tuning out, 10

Upper smile, 22

Verbal communication, nonverbal
    elements in, 7–8
Verbal tics, 73. *See also* Sounds.

Walking styles as body language,
    40–42
Weak handshake, 30
Woolbert, C.H., 48
Wringing of hands, 35
Wrinkling of nose, 21

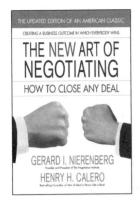

THE NEW ART OF NEGOTIATING

How to Close Any Deal

Gerard I. Nierenberg and Henry H. Calero

You negotiate every day of your life. Whether you are asking your employer for a raise or persuading your child to do his homework, everything is a negotiation. Written by Gerard Nierenberg, the world's foremost authority on the subject, *The New Art of Negotiating* is an updated, expanded version of the million-copy bestseller that introduced us all to the art of effective negotiation.

When *The Art of Negotiating* first appeared, it taught us that negotiation doesn't have to be an adversarial process that ends in victory for one party and defeat for his hapless rival. Since then, the landscape of business has changed greatly. *The New Art of Negotiating* provides Nierenberg's effective strategies redesigned for today's world. You will learn how to analyze your opponent's motivation, negotiate toward mutually satisfying terms, learn from your opponent's body language, and much more. Throughout, the author will guide you in successfully applying his famous "everybody wins" tactics to the bargaining process.

$15.95 • 208 pages • 6 x 9-inch quality paperback • ISBN 978-0-7570-0305-9

TALKING WITH YOUR HANDS, LISTENING WITH YOUR EYES

A Complete Photographic Guide to American Sign Language

Gabriel Grayson

After English and Spanish, it is the third most common language in North America. Over 22 million people use it to communicate. It has its own beauty, its own unmistakable form, and its own inherent culture. It is American Sign Language (ASL), the language of the deaf.

Talking With Your Hands explains signing basics, covering such topics as handshapes, fingerspelling, signing etiquette, and more. The remaining chapters provide over 1,700 words and phrases. Throughout the book, informative insets focus on fascinating aspects of deaf history, deaf culture, and significant deaf personalities.

$26.95 • 392 pages • 8.5 x 11-inch quality paperback • ISBN 978-0-7570-0007-2

SPEAKING SCARED, SOUNDING GOOD

Public Speaking for the Private Person

Peter Desberg, PhD

For millions, the idea of public speaking is terrifying—actually ranking ahead of the fear of death. Many books on public speaking promise to turn shy talkers into impressively confident speakers, but *Speaking Scared, Sounding Good* is different. Written by Dr. Peter Desberg, a practicing psychologist who has taught thousands of people to speak in front of groups, it doesn't make ridiculous claims. What it does do is provide you with proven techniques that will enable you to make it through any speech and—even though you may still be nervous—sound as if you know what you are talking about. You'll learn how to relax, how to focus, and how to set reachable goals for yourself. Through worksheets and self-tests, you'll be able to isolate and address your individual needs. The author even discusses the unique speaking problems associated with dyslexia.

If the fear of public speaking has been holding you back in your career—or if you've simply run out of excuses to avoid talking in front of your local garden club—*Speaking Scared, Sounding Good* will successfully guide you through the process.

$16.95 • 288 pages • 7.5 x 9-inch quality paperback • ISBN 978-0-7570-0262-5

OUR SECRET RULES

Why We Do the Things We Do

Jordan Weiss, MD

We all live according to rules that regulate our behaviors. Some rules—ones we are conscious of—are clear. Others, however, are unconscious, and when we do things that go against them, we experience stress, anxiety, apprehension, and emotional exhaustion—and we never know why. This book offers a unique system that helps uncover our most secret rules. Once we are aware of them, we can then learn to live within their boundaries, or we can attempt to change them.

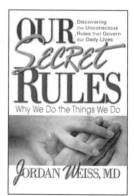

$12.95 • 240 pages • 6 x 9-inch quality paperback • ISBN 978-0-7570-0010-2